PHIL VICKERY

SAVE MONEY GOOD MONEY DIET

PHIL VICKERY

SAVE MONEY

MONEY GOOD

DIET

INTRODUCTION BY IAN MARBER

An Hachette UK Company
www.hachette.co.uk

First published in Great Britain in 2019 by
Kyle Books, an imprint of Kyle Cathie Ltd
Carmelite House
50 Victoria Embankment
London EC4Y 0DZ
www.kylebooks.co.uk

ISBN: 978 0 85783 787 5

Distributed in the US by Hachette Book Group, 1290 Avenue
of the Americas, 4th and 5th Floors, New York, NY 10104

Distributed in Canada by Canadian Manda Group, 664
Annette St., Toronto, Ontario, Canada M6S 2C8

This book is published to accompany the television series
Save Money Good Diet, first broadcast on ITV in 2019. Save
Money Good Diet is produced by Twofour.
Executive Producer: Rachel Innes-Lumsden
Series Producer: Colin May

Publisher: Joanna Copestick
Editorial Director: Judith Hannam
Project Editor: Claire Rogers
Editorial Assistant: Isabel Gonzalez-Prendergast
Design: Nicky Collings
Photographer: Tara Fisher
Food styling: Lottie Covell
Props styling: Linda Berlin
Nutritional analysis: Fiona Hunter
Production: Emily Noto

A Cataloguing in Publication record for this title is available
from the British Library

Printed and bound in Italy

10 9 8 7 6 5 4 3 2 1

CONTENTS

For a big part of my life I worked in top hotels and restaurants living the cooking dream. My sole goal in life was to achieve a coveted Michelin star. For that to happen you have to sacrifice a hell of a lot of your personal life. Forget about holidays, birthdays and days off: the job comes first. Work ceases to be a nine-to-five and becomes a complete way of life. I loved it and thrived on the twice daily deadline of being ready for a busy lunch and dinner. Once said star arrived, I was over the moon: it was like no other feeling in the world. Receiving a Michelin star catapulted me into a different league and after it came numerous other awards – including AA Rosettes, *The Times* Restaurant of the Year, Dessert Chef of the Year and Meat Chef of the Year.

A few years later, Mr Michelin, decided my food no longer warranted a star (even though the AA still gave me four Rosettes). I was devastated. At about the same time, we opened a brasserie serving relaxed, easy food for which you didn't need to dress up. That venue was buzzing. It was fun, lively and very busy. Many of our regular customers began to eat there rather than at the restaurant. The spend per head went up. At that point, I decided I wouldn't concern myself with Mr Michelin and would instead crack on with simple, tasty food. I have never looked back.

I have cooked on the telly for the best part of twenty-five years. I have never had a problem cooking with low-cost prepared ingredients – name me a chef who doesn't use frozen peas or tomato ketchup! At first the food purists (and certain well-known chefs) accused me of 'selling out', of de-skilling the industry. Even now I get the odd kicking on social media. But it didn't deter me. Although I will never compromise on flavour, I will always look for ways to save money and make cooking easier.

For this book (and the TV series) I have tried to cook everyday meals more healthily and with less money. I have cut down the calories, salt, fat, oil and sugar. I have also sought to reduce the amount of meat or fish protein, not only because we don't need as much as we think, but also because it's cheaper to use other, tasty alternatives.

This isn't a diet book: it lets you cook and enjoy food with a nod to being healthier and prudent. As my wife once said to me about the Michelin star experience, 'I don't want to worship the Great Food God'. Hear, hear to that. Oh, and by the way, the year I got my Michelin star, I cooked the head inspector a frozen, defrosted chicken and a sponge pudding with custard (made from powder) for dinner. I rest my case.

PHIL

GUIDE TO THIS BOOK

Included in this book are healthier – and cheaper –
versions of the **Nation's Top 10** dishes,
which are identified by the following graphic:

**NATION'S
FAVOURITE
DISH**

The cost of these dishes, and all the others
in the book, are based on Tesco prices,
as this is the UK's leading supermarket,
and were correct at the time of going to press.
The cost quoted is for the entire dish, not individual portions.

You can find the total cost under the name
of each recipe. it looks like this.

£4.18

EATING HEALTHILY ON A BUDGET

IAN MARBER

LONG-TERM RESEARCH TELLS US THAT A GOOD DIET CONTAINS LEAN PROTEIN, COMPLEX CARBOHYDRATES, LOTS OF FIBRE, SOME DAIRY AND, OF COURSE, PLENTY OF VEGETABLES AND FRUIT.

WHAT MAKES A GOOD DIET?

Since I qualified as a nutrition therapist in 1999, I have worked with thousands of people to help them make healthy food choices. Everyone has different reasons for seeking the guidance of a nutrition professional, ranging from a specific health concern, such as raised cholesterol or blood pressure, to skin issues such as eczema and, of course, managing their weight. But many people seek more general nutritional guidance just to make sure that they are making the best choices they can to support their general health and reduce the risk of illness using all that a good diet can deliver.

But what is a good diet? Long-term research tells us that it contains lean protein, complex carbohydrates, lots of fibre, some dairy and, of course, plenty of vegetables and fruit. In other words, including all the food groups, but none of the fads.

Proteins contain amino acids that are the building blocks for tissue, organs and muscle. While some foods fall into more than one category, broadly speaking protein can come from meats, fish and poultry and is found in plant-based foods such as nuts and seeds, lentils, chickpeas and other legumes, as well as tofu and mycoprotein.

COMPLEX CARBS

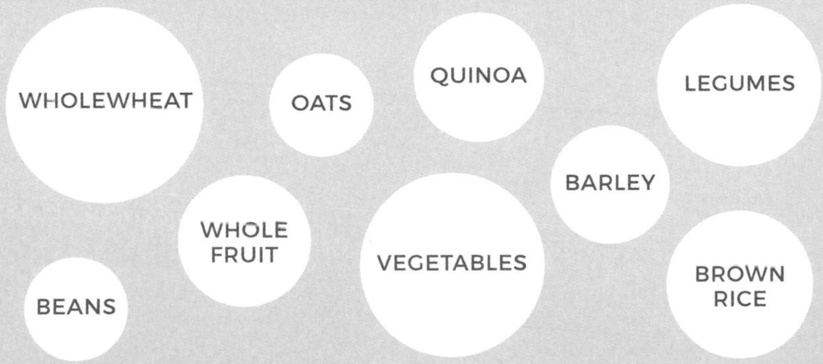

WHOLEWHEAT

OATS

QUINOA

LEGUMES

WHOLE FRUIT

BARLEY

BEANS

VEGETABLES

BROWN RICE

Carbohydrates are the human body's preferred source of fuel, as they are easily broken down by the digestive system. There are two types: simple and complex. Simple carbs tend to be processed foods, such as white grains, and are lacking in fibre. Complex carbohydrates are those that contain plenty of fibre and are found in many foods, notably whole grains including oats, wholewheat, brown rice and quinoa, but it is also found in whole fruit and vegetables, beans and legumes.

Fibre is an important part of a good diet for several reasons – it helps reduce excess cholesterol, encourages healthy gut bacteria and can help regulate levels of sugar, or glucose, in the blood.

**GOOD FATS,
SUCH AS
OMEGA-3, ARE
FOUND IN FISH,
HEMP AND CHIA
SEEDS, WALNUTS,
AVOCADOS,
PUMPKINS AND
SUNFLOWER
SEEDS AND
THEIR OILS.**

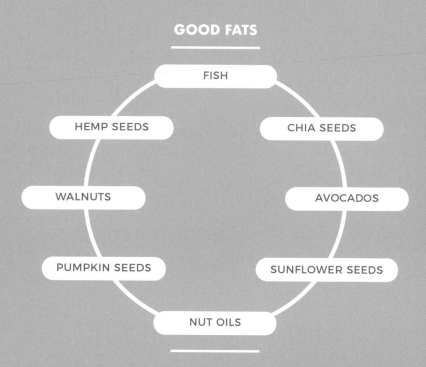

GOOD FATS

FISH

HEMP SEEDS

CHIA SEEDS

WALNUTS

AVOCADOS

PUMPKIN SEEDS

SUNFLOWER SEEDS

NUT OILS

As for fats, some are deemed to be beneficial and are referred to as essential, as they need to come from the diet. These good fats, such as omega-3, are found in fish, hemp and chia seeds, walnuts, avocados, pumpkins and sunflower seeds and their oils.

When it comes to unwanted fats, it's trans or hydrogenated fats, found in some processed foods including biscuits and confectionery, that we should avoid. Another fat, known as saturated fat, needs to be limited and is found in fatty cuts of red meat, processed meats such as sausages and salami, and high-fat dairy products such as cheese, ice cream and milk.

There are other foodstuffs that we need to limit, including salt, free sugars and unwanted types of fats, as we know that they can contribute to many potential health issues such as heart disease and obesity and can even increase the risk of developing type 2 diabetes.

The sugars we need to limit are free sugars, which are the sugars that are added to recipes, not those that are naturally occurring in fruits. For example, you'll find free sugars in sweets, cola and chocolate; but also, when fruit is juiced, removing the fibre, this frees up fructose, or fruit sugars, making them count as free sugars.

More than 6 grams of salt a day can disturb the balance between potassium and sodium, which in turn can raise blood pressure, a significant factor in heart disease.

SATURATED FAT NEEDS TO BE LIMITED AND IS FOUND IN FATTY CUTS OF RED MEAT, PROCESSED MEATS SUCH AS SAUSAGES AND SALAMI, AND HIGH-FAT DAIRY PRODUCTS.

40 PER CENT OF WHAT WE EAT EVERY DAY SHOULD BE FRUIT AND VEGETABLES, 38 PER CENT, SHOULD BE WHOLEGRAINS AND COMPLEX CARBS, PROTEIN AT 12 PER CENT, DAIRY 8 PER CENT AND OILS AT 1 PER CENT

GETTING PORTION SIZES RIGHT

Getting the balance right between the food groups is another aspect we need to consider when eating a good diet. In 2016, Public Health England updated their nutrition advice, which suggests that around 40 per cent of what we eat every day should be fruit and vegetables, a little less, 38 per cent, should be wholegrains and complex carbs, protein should be 12 per cent, dairy and alternatives around 8 per cent and lastly oils and spreads at 1 per cent.

DAILY FOOD CONSUMPTION

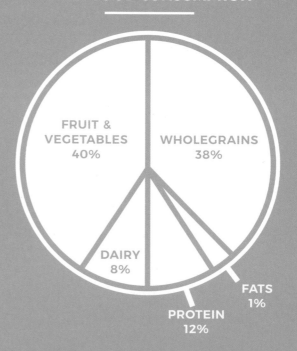

FRUIT & VEGETABLES 40%

WHOLEGRAINS 38%

DAIRY 8%

PROTEIN 12%

FATS 1%

Thinking about a main course, I often advise my clients that they should have a serving of protein a little smaller than a tightly clenched fist, then enough vegetables to cover their hand with the fingers spread out, while whole grains would take up a little less than half to a third of the same space.

But what about calories? Even the best diet can be undermined by eating too much, and so calories should be limited to around 2,000 a day for an adult woman, while for a man that figure rises to 2,500. The last part of a good diet is making sure that what we eat stays within those guidelines yet still delivers all the nutrition we need.

STAYING ON TRACK

So far, so good. Yet after twenty years advising clients about healthy food, I know that there are many challenges that we might face when we make improvements to our diet that have less to do with food groups and nutrients but involve how we like to live our lives. In my experience, there are three that come up time and time again.

Firstly, we have to like what we eat. We are so lucky to live in a time when we have access to foods of all types, and as enjoying food is an important part of a healthy diet, what we eat has to appeal to us. I am sure many of us have embarked on a healthy eating plan, starting off with gusto and enthusiasm only to give it up after a while because it's just not suiting us, especially if we don't like the food even though it may be a healthy choice.

The answer is to eat foods that we like   familiar dishes that deliver on flavour and texture, ones that are a pleasure to eat so that you can keep enjoying them often.

2500
CALORIES
PER DAY

2000
CALORIES
PER DAY

> **A GOOD DIET COMES FROM MAKING CONSISTENTLY HEALTHY CHOICES AT LEAST 80 PER CENT OF THE TIME.**

PLANNING FOR REAL LIFE

Secondly, our chosen plan has to be something that we can follow in the real world. It has to fit in with our lives, perhaps with a couple of compromises but even with them, our diet has to suit our individual situations.

If the diet plan means that we can't share a meal with friends or family, have to avoid eating out, or are limited on time, then aside from making us miserable, we are likely to fall off the wagon all too soon.

Similarly, a good diet comes from making consistently healthy choices at least 80 per cent of the time. While making the occasional good diet choice may go some way towards supporting your health, the true benefits are enjoyed with an overall good diet.

GOOD DIET ON A BUDGET

Thirdly, we need to ensure that our healthy diet is affordable. I have found that if the foods in whichever plan we choose are hard to find, exotic or pricey, this makes the diet really hard to stick with. We might start off with great intentions, but once real life kicks in – and it always does – once again there's a greater risk that we will run out of steam if it all becomes too much. If our plan means that we are spending more on food than we would normally do, then it's harder to keep up. We might make allowances here, but what happens when life throws up extra expenses, maybe some home improvements, holidays to save for or a boiler that needs replacing? These things become more important, and so the diet gets ditched.

COOKING QUALITY FOOD

As you can see, there are a few elements that make up a good diet, and so a plan that fulfils our nutritional needs – one with plenty of fibre, complex carbs, protein and good fats without excess salt, sugars or fat – yet is enjoyable, practical and affordable gets my attention.

The varied and practical recipes that follow make the best of good foods so that you get your calories from quality sources. They tick all the nutritional boxes, which means that you get more bang for your buck without overeating or having to sacrifice flavour.

I jumped at the chance to write this introduction to Phil Vickery's new book, as *Save Money Good Diet* is all these things, delivered by clever recipes created with every element of a good diet in mind.

MAKE THE BEST OF GOOD FOOD SO THAT YOU GET YOUR CALORIES FROM QUALITY SOURCES.

BREAKFAST & BRUNCH

Using chicken sausages is a good substitute for pork, as they contain less fat – look for low-fat versions to make this even healthier.

For me, this is one of the most difficult meals to cut down on the calories. I mean, who can resist a great fry-up? Well, it can be done by boxing a bit clever. For instance, instead of hash browns I use frozen mash pellets (or leftover roast or boiled spuds) mixed with leftover or frozen vegetables. Using mustard means no salt is needed. Cutting the fat off half the bacon, plus grilling open mushrooms with just a mist of oil all helps to reduce the fat content. Poaching eggs rather than frying and using reduced salt and sugar baked beans are another way to cut down calories.

ENERGY (KCALS)	PROTEIN	FAT	SATURATED FAT	CARB.	TOTAL SUGARS	SALT	FIBRE
552	59.5	24	8	21	5	4.4	6

SERVES	PREP TIME	COOK TIME
4	30 MINS	20 MINS

Preheat the oven to 200°C/gas 6. Preheat the grill to high.

Place the mash in a bowl with the leftover vegetables, mustard powder and a little pepper and mix well. Add a dash of skimmed milk, if needed, to loosen – not too much. Form the mixture into four round patties and chill in the fridge to firm up for 10 minutes.

Meanwhile, fry the chicken sausages in a dry, non-stick pan, rolling occasionally to get a nice even colour.

Place the bacon, tomatoes and mushrooms under the grill. Lightly spray the mushrooms with a little oil and season with a dash of pepper. Grill everything, turning when needed, and take out each item when cooked.

In a small pan, heat the baked beans.

Put a couple of sprays of oil in a non-stick frying pan over a high heat and colour the patties on both sides. Transfer to a baking tray and pop in the oven for 15 minutes.

Add a dash of vinegar to a pan of unsalted water, and then bring to a hard boil. Carefully break in the eggs, one by one. Wait until the boiling water has sealed the eggs, and then lower the heat to a simmer and cook for a further 2 minutes. Remove from the heat and leave for 2–3 minutes to let the egg whites cook through.

Once everything is cooked and the patties are warmed through, divide everything between four plates and serve.

100g frozen mash pellets, defrosted (or leftover mashed potatoes)

250g leftover vegetables (from your Sunday roast, ideally including cabbage), finely chopped

½ teaspoon mustard powder

2–3 tablespoons skimmed milk (optional)

8 low-fat chicken sausages

8 rashers back bacon, fat removed from 4 (freeze the fat for use at a later date)

4 fresh tomatoes, halved lengthways

4 large, flat mushrooms

rapeseed oil (in a spray bottle)

400g can reduced sugar and salt baked beans

8 medium eggs

freshly ground black pepper

CLOUD EGGS

£0.57

I have to say I was a little sceptical when I first tried these: they seemed a bit of a fad, but now, having cooked them many times, I really like them as a great alternative to poached or fried eggs. One of the great points of this dish is the fact that you only need to serve two and as long as you bulk out with a little bread or a few toppings of your choice, you do have a very nice healthy breakfast or light snack. I tend to serve them with lightly toasted pumpernickel or sourdough to add a bit of body to the dish.

SERVES	PREP TIME	COOK TIME		ENERGY (KCALS)	PROTEIN	FAT	SATURATED FAT	CARB.	TOTAL SUGARS	SALT	FIBRE
2	5 MINS	6–8 MINS		160	15.5	11	3	0	0	0.96	0

4 medium eggs, at room
   temperature, separated
pinch of table salt
pinch of ground pepper
½ pinch of cream of tartar

Preheat the oven to 230°C/gas 8.

Place the egg whites into a mixing bowl. Add a pinch of salt and pepper and half a pinch of cream of tartar. Whisk using a hand-held electric whisk at a medium speed until thick, glossy and creamy.

Spoon four mounds of egg white onto a baking tray lined with greaseproof paper. Using a small spoon, make a small indent in the top of the meringue. Bake in the oven straight away for 4–5 minutes.

Once lightly browned and well puffed up, remove the tray from the oven and add the egg yolks to the indent. Return to the oven for 2–3 minutes, just to warm the yolk through. Do not overcook or the meringue will collapse and shrivel slightly, giving the whites a chewy texture. Serve straight away; you will be surprised how firm the meringue is.

These are nice served on toasted pumpernickel, sourdough or even English muffins.

Fillings can be added before cooking the meringue, once the whites are cooked, or sprinkled over the cooked eggs just before serving. Try some crispy smoked bacon, sun-dried tomatoes, Parmesan, finely chopped avocado and red onion, chopped basil or coriander, chopped chipolatas or smoked salmon strips.

I serve this as part of a breakfast offering or as a dessert, and it goes down equally well. You can use any fruit you like, but add it at the last moment to keep the freshness and stop the fruit going soggy. I sometimes use two pots of single-serving microwaveable instant porridge purely for convenience, though they're a little more expensive.

STRAWBERRY PORRIDGE

£4.03

ENERGY (KCALS)	PROTEIN	FAT	SATURATED FAT	CARB.	TOTAL SUGARS	SALT	FIBRE
179	3	8.5	8.5	20.5	14.5	0.05	4.5

SERVES	PREP TIME	COOK TIME
4	15 MINS	5 MINS IN MICROWAVE

Place the porridge into a bowl and mix with the crème fraîche. Add the honey and just swirl through. Add the lime zest and juice and the strawberries and again, just swirl through. Serve.

250g cooked cold porridge (made with skimmed milk or water – no salt), broken up with a fork

200g half- or reduced-fat crème fraîche

2–3 tablespoons runny honey

zest and juice of 2 small limes

400g fresh strawberries, hulled and cut into 4

TIP

Using reduced-fat crème fraîche is a great way to limit your intake of saturated fat; you can also use yogurt – or even quark – as low-fat alternatives.

This recipe is from a friend of mine, Kirsty Keiller. She is a personal trainer and swears by these for eating anytime of the day, but they are especially good at breakfast. I thought they may need some flour, but after cooking them a few times I realised they are perfect without any at all. They are sweet enough to serve on their own, but you could serve them with a little grilled back bacon – or even a couple of chipolatas.

FLOURLESS BANANA WAFFLES

£1.23

ENERGY (KCALS)	PROTEIN	FAT	SATURATED FAT	CARB.	TOTAL SUGARS	SALT	FIBRE
151	7	4.5	1.5	20	17	0.6	1.4

SERVES	PREP TIME	COOK TIME
4	10 MINS	10 MINS

Break up the bananas in a bowl with a fork, but do not mash too finely. Add the baking powder and spice and mix well, then add the eggs and break up with a fork.

Spray a 24cm non-stick frying pan over a medium heat with a little oil. Spoon the mix into four waffles close to the edge and cook for 2–3 minutes until just starting to bubble at the edge. Alternatively, cook in a waffle iron if you have one.

Turn the heat down and cover with a tight-fitting lid or foil. Cook for 5–6 minutes until the centres are still a little wobbly but the outside is set.

Carefully flip over and cook, uncovered, for a further 2 minutes until fully cooked through.

4 ripe bananas

1½ teaspoons baking powder

½ teaspoon mixed spice

3 medium eggs

vegetable oil (in a spray bottle)

NUTTY WAFFLES WITH AVOCADO

£4.02

A nice twist on what is pretty much a staple breakfast offering these days. The balance of nuts, avocado, vinegar and my current favourite herb, Thai basil, really works well. Once cooked, they also freeze really well.

	SERVES	PREP TIME	COOK TIME	ENERGY (KCALS)	PROTEIN	FAT	SATURATED FAT	CARB.	TOTAL SUGARS	SALT	FIBRE
	4	15 MINS	10 MINS	523	11.5	39	6.5	28	4.5	0.9	6

2 medium eggs, separated

115g self-raising flour

75g pecans or Brazil nuts, finely chopped

150–175ml cold skimmed milk

2 tablespoons extra virgin olive oil, plus 1 teaspoon for frying

For the topping

2 medium ripe avocados, peeled, destoned and sliced

½ small red onion, very finely chopped

1–2 tablespoons balsamic vinegar

2 tablespoons finely chopped Thai basil

extra virgin olive oil

salt and freshly ground black pepper

Place all the ingredients for the topping into a bowl and mix well. Season with a little salt and pepper and set aside.

Place the egg yolks, flour and pecans or Brazil nuts into a bowl with a pinch of salt. Mix well, then add 150ml milk and mix together. Add a touch more milk if the mixture is too tight, then finally stir in the olive oil.

In a separate bowl, whisk the egg whites until they are soft and foamy and then fold into the flour and yolk mixture.

Lightly oil a large, non-stick, flat griddle pan or a waffle iron over a medium heat. Add the mixture and cook until light and golden. (If using a griddle pan, turn out the waffle and cut into four.) Spoon on the avocado mix and serve.

TIP

Avocados are a great source of potassium, which is an essential mineral for a healthy body, plus it can enhance your metabolism. Or you can try topping these waffles with lightly poached eggs for an extra hit of protein.

Here is a different angle on a breakfast wrap. I tend to make the pancakes and omelettes the day before and gently warm in a microwave on half power, then add the ham and cheese, roll up and serve. I sometimes use crispy bacon and/or thinly cut grilled sausages, but the choice really is yours. I warn you, one batch is never enough.

BUCKWHEAT HAM & EGG ROLLS

£4.72

ENERGY (KCALS)	PROTEIN	FAT	SATURATED FAT	CARB.	TOTAL SUGARS	SALT	FIBRE
438	37	23	8.5	20	3	2.3	0.7

SERVES	PREP TIME	COOK TIME
4	35 MINS	15 MINS

Make the pancake batter by placing the eggs, salt, a little pepper and the buckwheat flour into a bowl with half the milk. Whisk until you have a fine batter, then add the rest of the milk and the chives and mix well.

Heat ½ tablespoon of the oil in a roughly 14cm non-stick frying pan over a high heat. Pour in a quarter of the batter and swirl around to cover the bottom of the pan. Cook for 1–2 minutes to get some colour, then flip and cook for a further 1 minute. Turn out onto a board and repeat until you have four pancakes.

For the filling, whisk the eggs and pour a quarter of the mixture into the frying pan. Cook a small omelette, the same size as the pancakes, then repeat until you have four omelettes.

Lay one omelette on top of each pancake, then sprinkle over some ham and mozzarella slices, and season well with salt and pepper. Roll up and serve.

For the pancakes
2 medium eggs
pinch of salt
80g buckwheat flour
175ml skimmed milk
4 tablespoons chopped chives
2 tablespoons any oil
freshly ground black pepper

For the filling
4 medium eggs
200g wafer-thin ham slices
250g reduced-fat mozzarella, sliced

TIP

Despite its name, buckwheat flour is actually wheat-free. It's also higher in fibre and protein than white flour, which keeps you feeling full for longer.

FETA, MINT & COURGETTE FRITTATA

£3.55

A great breakfast or brunch dish, this can be made the day before and gently reheated in a moderate oven or microwave. I tend to add watercress, but rocket and spinach also all work well. For a really healthy option you could add all three! I use a small amount of feta to give the acidic kick that this frittata needs.

SERVES	PREP TIME	COOK TIME		ENERGY (KCALS)	PROTEIN	FAT	SATURATED FAT	CARB.	TOTAL SUGARS	SALT	FIBRE
4	15 MINS	20 MINS		343	22.5	17.5	6.5	21.5	7	1.3	6

1 tablespoon olive oil

2 onions, very finely chopped

2 garlic cloves, finely chopped

1 large courgette, chopped into 1cm pieces

200g frozen petit pois, defrosted

200g cooked potatoes, skin on, cut into 2cm cubes

100g feta cheese, crumbled

2 tablespoons finely chopped fresh mint

1 small bunch of watercress, rocket or spinach (or all three), roughly chopped

6 medium eggs

salt and freshly ground black pepper

Preheat the oven to 200°C/gas 6.

Heat the oil in a large, non-stick, ovenproof frying pan over a medium heat, then add the onions, garlic and courgettes and cook for 10 minutes to soften. Sprinkle over the peas, cooked potatoes, feta, mint and watercress, rocket or spinach evenly.

Whisk the eggs together and season with salt (not too much as the cheese is quite salty) and pepper. Pour the eggs over the warm vegetables and cheese, then bake in the oven for 15–20 minutes to cook the egg. Do not overcook, or the frittata will soufflé.

Remove the pan from the oven, cover with foil and leave for 10 minutes to set. Once cooled, chill well.

RICOTTA-STUFFED TOMATOES

£5.77

A nice and easy breakfast dish that can be made the night before, then grilled or baked when you are ready. I sometimes use cottage cheese or even mozzarella and serve with poached eggs, or that perennial favourite mashed avocado, on the sourdough.

SERVES	PREP TIME	COOK TIME		ENERGY (KCALS)	PROTEIN	FAT	SATURATED FAT	CARB.	TOTAL SUGARS	SALT	FIBRE
4	25 MINS	8-10 MINS		268	10	12	4.5	29	6	0.8	3.5

2 tablespoons olive oil

150g baby spinach leaves

200g ricotta

squeeze of lemon juice

pinch of freshly grated nutmeg

4 large, ripe beef tomatoes

4 thick slices grilled sourdough

salt and freshly ground black
   pepper

Preheat the grill to a medium–high heat, or heat an oven to 220°C/gas 7.

Heat the oil in a pan over a medium heat and add the spinach. Season with a little salt and pepper and cook for 2–3 minutes until wilted, stirring constantly. Transfer to a colander to drain off the excess water.

Place the ricotta into a bowl, add a squeeze of lemon juice and the nutmeg and mix really well. Slice the top off each tomato and discard. Being careful not to damage the skin, scoop out the seeds and flesh and add to the ricotta along with the drained spinach, then mix well.

Place the tomatoes into a baking dish and divide the ricotta and spinach mixture between them, filling them nice and proud. Grill or bake the stuffed tomatoes for 6–8 minutes until the tomatoes have slightly softened but still hold their shape and the filling is heated through. Serve with slices of grilled sourdough.

TIP

You don't need to use much salt in this dish, as the ricotta, lemon and pepper add all the seasoning needed.

Fish contains much less saturated fat than meat, and salmon in particular is full of omega-3 fatty acids and vitamin D. I use seed mustard here because it packs such a punch of flavour that you don't need to add any salt.

MARYLAND-STYLE CRAB CAKES

£10.25

There is no potato in these little beauties and they are really easy to make. The texture is soft and succulent, so be careful how you handle them in preparation and cooking. You can use canned, fresh or frozen crabmeat depending on your preference and budget. I top them with poached or soft-boiled eggs and a rather unusual cucumber relish that works perfectly.

SERVES	PREP TIME	COOK TIME	ENERGY (KCALS)	PROTEIN	FAT	SATURATED FAT	CARB.	TOTAL SUGARS	SALT	FIBRE
4	20 MINS	20 MINS	565	42	31.5	5	28	15.5	2.3	0.8

1 medium egg

1 tablespoon mayonnaise

2 teaspoons English mustard

dash of Worcestershire sauce

200g brown crabmeat

4–6 tablespoons dried breadcrumbs

400g white crab meat

4 spring onions, finely chopped

2 tablespoons any oil

cornflower or arrowroot powder

4 hot poached eggs

salt and freshly ground black pepper

Place the egg, mayonnaise, mustard and Worcestershire sauce into a bowl. Add the brown crabmeat and breadcrumbs and mix well. Add the white crabmeat and spring onions and gently stir in, not breaking up the meat too much. Season well with salt and pepper. Mould into small patties and chill in the fridge for 1 hour.

Heat the oil in a frying pan over a medium heat. Remove the patties from the fridge, dust with a little cornflour or arrowroot powder and gently fry on each side for 3–4 minutes. Serve with a poached egg and the relish (below).

Cucumber relish

75ml white wine vinegar

50g caster sugar

2 tablespoons black onion seeds

pinch of dried chilli flakes

1 cucumber, frozen whole and defrosted

½ garlic clove, finely crushed

4 tablespoons extra virgin olive oil

Place the vinegar, sugar, onion seeds, chilli flakes and a pinch of salt and pepper into a saucepan with 100ml of water and simmer for 5–6 minutes until you have a nice syrupy texture. Set aside to cool.

Slice the cucumber into 5mm slices lengthways, then into 5mm strips. Pat really dry with a kitchen towel, then place the strips into a bowl, along with the garlic. Add the cooled dressing and mix well, then add the olive oil and mix again. It's best to leave overnight, if possible. Season again just before you serve.

TIP

By cutting out the potato here, you can get away with only a few tablespoons of breadcrumbs to hold everything together, resulting in these low-carb, protein-rich cakes.

TIP

If you don't have time to prepare sweet potato in the morning, you can use the equivalent weight of frozen cubes cooked straight from the freezer.

Having just returned from Mexico, I had to have a recipe for refried beans somewhere. I just love the texture and flavour they add to a dish. In fact, I sometimes have refried beans, fried eggs and chopped avocado for breakfast. You can make your own refried beans, but that can take quite a long time with soaking and cooking, so I normally buy canned.

SWEET POTATO & REFRIED BEAN TACO

£5.12

ENERGY (KCALS)	PROTEIN	FAT	SATURATED FAT	CARB.	TOTAL SUGARS	SALT	FIBRE
542	13	23	6	65	15	1.75	11

SERVES	PREP TIME	COOK TIME
4	30 MINS	45 MINS

Place the red onion into a bowl, then add the vinegar and season with salt and pepper. Mix well and leave for 20 minutes.

Meanwhile, heat the oil in a frying pan over a high heat, then add the onion, chilli and garlic and fry for 2–3 minutes, or until they take on a little colour.

Add the sweet potatoes, stock cube and 50ml of water and bring to the boil. Cover and boil for 12–15 minutes, or until the sweet potato is soft, then uncover to allow the moisture to escape. Remove from the heat, season well with salt and pepper and then fold through the coriander.

Lay out the tacos and spread with a little of the warm refried beans. Add a little lettuce, then top with the sweet potato mix. Top with chopped avocado, a dot of crème fraîche and some drained pickled onions.

For the onion

1 small red onion, very thinly sliced
6 tablespoons cider vinegar
salt and freshly ground black pepper

For the sweet potato

4 tablespoons any oil
1 red onion, finely chopped
¼ teaspoon dried red chilli flakes
3 garlic cloves, finely chopped
2 small sweet potatoes (approx. 400g), peeled and finely chopped
½ × 10g vegetable stock cube
4 tablespoons chopped fresh coriander

To serve

4 large wheat tortillas
200g refried beans (canned is fine), warmed
finely shredded iceberg or romaine lettuce
1 small ripe avocado, finely chopped
75g reduced-fat crème fraîche

SOUPS & SALADS

SIMPLE CHICKEN SOUP

£4.02

This soup needs no oil or salt, and there's no need to sauté anything; you just simmer away and then add the spinach. I add yeast extract and miso to bring out the flavour of all the veg and chicken, but be careful as a little goes a long way. You can, of course, add more veg or a different protein such as pork or turkey if you prefer.

SERVES	PREP TIME	COOK TIME
4	20 MINS	25-30 MINS

ENERGY (KCALS)	PROTEIN	FAT	SATURATED FAT	CARB.	TOTAL SUGARS	SALT	FIBRE
183	25	3	1	11	9	1.3	5

2 medium onions, finely chopped

4 garlic cloves, finely chopped

2 large carrots, peeled and finely chopped

4 celery sticks, finely chopped

250g chestnut mushrooms

400g skinless chicken thighs, bone in

10g reduced-salt chicken stock cube

1 teaspoon yeast extract

1 teaspoon miso paste

150g baby spinach leaves

freshly ground black pepper

Place 1 litre of water into a large saucepan. Add the onions, garlic, carrots, celery and mushrooms. Bring to the boil.

Remove the bone from the chicken thighs by carefully slicing down each side of the bone with a sharp knife and cutting around both knuckles. Place the bones and meat in the pan with the vegetables. Next add the stock cube, yeast extract, miso and some pepper and simmer for a few minutes. Bring to the boil, then simmer for 20 minutes.

Check the seasoning and adjust if needed. Fish out the four thigh bones, stir in the spinach to wilt and serve.

This is an easy boil-up recipe; I have reduced the meat and added more barley and vegetables to reduce the fat content. One whole stock cube is used, so you don't need to add any salt – you just need some pepper and parsley to finish. This broth tastes even better warmed up the next day.

SCOTCH BROTH

£8.34

ENERGY (KCALS)	PROTEIN	FAT	SATURATED FAT	CARB.	TOTAL SUGARS	SALT	FIBRE
349	30	11	4.5	30	13	1.2	10

SERVES	PREP TIME	COOK TIME
4	20 MINS	2 HRS

Place the lamb and about 1.5 litres of water together into a pan and bring to the boil. Once boiling, reduce the heat and simmer for 10 minutes, removing any scum or fat that rises to the surface.

Add the barley, stock cube and all the vegetables and simmer for 1 hour 30 minutes, or until the lamb is tender.

Taste and adjust the seasoning, if needed, then add the parsley and serve.

450g leg of lamb or mutton, all fat removed, cut into small cubes
75g pearl barley
10g reduced-salt vegetable stock cube
4 large carrots, peeled and cubed
2 large leeks, cut into small pieces
2 large onions, cut into small pieces
2 small turnips, cut into small pieces
6 celery sticks, cut into small pieces
freshly chopped parsley
freshly ground black pepper

TIP

Lamb meat is a high-quality source of protein, and leg of lamb or mutton tends to have less fat than shoulder.

When I was training, the soups fell into two categories: thick puréed ones such as leek and potato or ham and leek; or consommé, a clear stock that was made predominantly from meat or fowl. It took days to make and was a bit of a faff. Nowadays, I'm really into intensely flavoured, simple, light stocks or broths; not only are they really good for you, but also they always hit the spot. Broths like this one are great all year round, light and fresh in the summer months and warm and filling in the winter months.

FRAGRANT PRAWN BROTH

£7.02

ENERGY (KCALS)	PROTEIN	FAT	SATURATED FAT	CARB.	TOTAL SUGARS	SALT	FIBRE
260	20.5	7.5	1	24	7	1.7	8

SERVES	PREP TIME	COOK TIME
4	15 MINS	15 MINS

Heat the oil in a large sauté pan over a high heat. Add the shallots, garlic, ginger, broccoli stalks and mange tout and cook for 2 minutes.

Add the boiling water, stock cube and tamarind juice and bring to the boil. Cook for 1 minute, then add the cooked broccoli florets, spinach, prawns and potato, if using, and cook for 2–3 minutes until the prawns are just cooked through.

Mix the cornflower, starch or arrowroot with 4 tablespoons of cold water and spoon into the broth. Stir until nicely thickened but not too much: you don't want a thick soup consistency. Remove the pan from the heat and stir in the coriander, basil and lime juice, then season with salt, pepper and a little sugar, if using. Serve with steamed basmati rice.

2 tablespoons any oil

2 medium shallots, finely sliced

2 garlic cloves, finely chopped

1 heaped tablespoon finely chopped fresh ginger

1 head of broccoli, stalk cut into 2.5cm cubes, head cut into very small florets and just cooked

150g mange tout, finely sliced

600–700ml boiling water

10g chicken stock cube, crumbled

1 tablespoon tamarind juice

100g baby spinach leaves

250g peeled freshwater prawns, halved

200g boiled potato, cooled and cut into 1cm cubes (optional)

2 tablespoons cornflour, tapioca starch or arrowroot powder

2 tablespoons each chopped fresh coriander and chopped fresh Thai basil

juice of 2 limes

sugar (optional)

salt and freshly ground black pepper

CHUNKY VEGETABLE BROTH

£3.69

A very easy broth that can be made in bulk and frozen. The more veg the better: even a can or two of veg or a few frozen beans such as broad or soya would not go amiss. I prefer not to liquidise too many soups as I really like to see all the components. I usually add a little Parmesan cheese and extra virgin olive oil as an optional extra here, but that's up to you.

SERVES	PREP TIME	COOK TIME		ENERGY (KCALS)	PROTEIN	FAT	SATURATED FAT	CARB.	TOTAL SUGARS	SALT	FIBRE
4	20 MINS	40-45 MINS		346	10.5	15	3.5	37	20	1.6	11

2 medium onions, chopped

4 medium carrots, peeled and chopped

4 garlic cloves, chopped

4 celery sticks, chopped

1 courgette, chopped

1 small Savoy (or any cabbage), finely sliced

400g can chopped tomatoes with herbs

10g vegetable stock cube

75g pearl barley

2 tablespoons grated Parmesan cheese (optional)

4–5 tablespoons extra virgin olive oil

salt (optional)

freshly ground black pepper

Place all the vegetables into a large saucepan; bear in mind that they will cook down to 50 per cent of the original volume, so don't panic if it looks like too much in the pan.

Add the tomatoes, 500ml of water, the stock cube and the barley and bring to the boil, then stir well. Reduce the heat and simmer for 40–45 minutes, or until the barley is cooked.

Once cooked, the broth should be thick and chunky. Taste, adjust the seasoning if needed, then add the cheese, if using, and stir through the olive oil.

HERB & SPRING ONION STOCK

£9.14

A cleansing, tasty, simple soup, perfect for a light meal or snack. I sometimes add a little yeast extract rather than miso; you can do this if you want a slightly different flavour profile. One thing you must do is add all the herbs at the last minute to keep their flavour and aroma, or place the herbs in your serving bowls and pour over the stock when ready to serve.

SERVES	PREP TIME	COOK TIME
2	10	10
	MINS	MINS

ENERGY (KCALS)	PROTEIN	FAT	SATURATED FAT	CARB.	TOTAL SUGARS	SALT	FIBRE
268	8	26.5	4.5	24.5	15.5	4.2	10.5

2 × 10g reduced-salt vegetable stock cubes

2 tablespoons miso paste

2 large carrots, peeled and cubed

8 spring onions, thinly sliced on a diagonal

1 bunch (approx. 100g) each of parsley, tarragon, coriander and basil (preferably Thai), roughly chopped

4–6 tablespoons good-quality extra virgin olive oil

freshly ground black pepper

Place 1.2 litres of water with the stock cubes and miso into a pan and bring to the boil. Reduce the heat, add the carrot and boil for 10 minutes, or until soft.

Add the spring onion and turn off the heat. Just before serving, add all the herbs, season with pepper and drizzle in the olive oil. Serve in deep bowls.

TIP

Miso is a fermented food rich in essential minerals as well as several B vitamins; combine this with the health benefits of the herbs used in this recipe (from better sleep and digestion to lower blood sugar and cholesterol) and this recipe packs a nutritional punch.

This is the easiest recipe going: just place everything into a saucepan and bring to the boil! You don't need to add salt here, because you are using a stock cube, plus the sun-dried tomatoes are nicely seasoned in their own oil. I think that cooking the onions and garlic first has no impact on the end result flavour-wise. Microwave rice is easy to use if you don't mind spending a little bit more. If you are using raw rice, allow about 100–120g and boil the soup until the rice is cooked before blitzing.

EASIEST TOMATO SOUP

£5.40

ENERGY (KCALS)	PROTEIN	FAT	SATURATED FAT	CARB.	TOTAL SUGARS	SALT	FIBRE
410	5.5	27	4	34	9	2.2	3

SERVES	PREP TIME	COOK TIME
4	15 MINS	10 MINS

Place everything into a saucepan and cover with about 600ml cold water. Bring to the boil, and then gently simmer for 12–15 minutes.

Blitz either in a blender or with a stick blender: I like to leave it quite chunky. That's it!

2 medium onions, very finely chopped

400g fresh baby plum tomatoes, halved

200g sun-dried tomatoes (and their oil)

2 garlic cloves, crushed

1 small bunch of fresh basil

10g reduced-salt vegetable stock cube

250g microwave pack long grain rice

2 tablespoons any vinegar

freshly ground black pepper

TIP

Tomatoes contain a phytonutrient called lycopene, which can benefit your heart, blood pressure and skin. Plus, when tomato is cooked, the level of lycopene doubles.

TUSCAN BEAN SOUP (RIBOLLITA)

£6.38

This soup was cooked for me in Italy years ago, and the chef who made it swore by the recipe. The only thing she did that I haven't included here was to soak dried beans overnight, then cook them and keep their water to use as the base of the soup. Plus she placed the bread in the bowls first and then spooned over the thick broth. This recipe is a cracker and tastes even better reheated the next day.

SERVES	PREP TIME	COOK TIME
4	20-25 MINS	20-25 MINS

ENERGY (KCALS)	PROTEIN	FAT	SATURATED FAT	CARB.	TOTAL SUGARS	SALT	FIBRE
448	19	12	2	55	16	0.7	21

2 × 400g cans cannellini beans, drained

2 tablespoons olive oil

2 onions, finely chopped

pinch of chilli flakes

4 garlic cloves, finely chopped

1 tablespoon tomato purée

4 small ripe tomatoes, roughly chopped

2 carrots, peeled and finely chopped

4 celery sticks, finely chopped

1 medium leek, finely chopped

2 teaspoons fresh thyme leaves

3 sprigs rosemary

10g stock cube

1 small Savoy cabbage, finely shredded

200g cavolo nero, finely shredded (optional)

freshly ground black pepper

To serve

4 slices bread (possibly Pugliese, Ciabatta will do), sliced

2 garlic cloves, peeled

good-quality extra virgin olive oil

Place one can of beans into a food-processor and blitz until you have a nice purée.

Heat the olive oil in a pan over a medium heat and add the onions, chilli and garlic, then cook for 3–4 minutes to soften. Add the tomato purée and fresh tomatoes and mix well, breaking the tomatoes down a little with the back of a spoon. Add the carrots, celery, leek, thyme, rosemary, puréed beans and enough water to cover everything by 2cm. Bring to the boil, add the stock cube and then simmer for 10 minutes, or until the carrots are just cooked.

Add the cabbage, cavolo nero, if using, and the other can of beans, and simmer for a further 10 minutes until the cabbage is just cooked. The soup should be so packed with vegetables and beans at this point, the wooden spoon should almost stand up on its own. Season with pepper and remove the rosemary stalks.

Pour the soup into deep bowls and serve with a little crisp bread rubbed with some fresh garlic. I like to add a dash of good-quality extra virgin olive oil to the top of the soup when serving.

There really is something immensely pleasing about eating a salad with a spoon. Yes, all the work is in the preparation, but it's so much easier to eat and I think psychologically you feel like you are eating more than just a salad. Pretty much anything goes, including frozen vegetables, canned beans and pulses, plus rice or even cooked and cooled pasta. Do make use of microwaveable rice, quinoa and wild and brown rice packets if you don't mind spending a little more.

'LEFT OVER' CHICKEN SALAD

£9.08

ENERGY (KCALS)	PROTEIN	FAT	SATURATED FAT	CARB.	TOTAL SUGARS	SALT	FIBRE		SERVES	PREP TIME
370	30	15	2.5	23	10	1	10		4	20
										MINS

Carefully mix together the cucumber, onions, lettuce, celery, radishes and tomatoes. Add the peas, borlotti beans, sweetcorn, mint, coriander and chicken, and mix well.

To make the dressing, place all the ingredients into a bowl with a dash of water and whisk together. Pour over the chilled salad and mix really well with a little salt and pepper. Serve straight away with spoons.

½ large cucumber, finely chopped

6 spring onions, finely chopped

2 Little Gem lettuce, finely chopped

4 celery sticks, finely chopped

8 radishes, finely chopped

4 large, ripe vine tomatoes, finely chopped

150g frozen peas, defrosted

400g can borlotti beans, drained

365g can sweetcorn, drained

4 tablespoons chopped fresh mint

4 tablespoons chopped fresh coriander

250g cooked chicken

salt and freshly ground black pepper

Dressing

3 tablespoons extra virgin olive oil

2 tablespoons low-fat mayonnaise

4 tablespoons sherry vinegar

2 tablespoons Dijon mustard

TIP

Frozen vegetables are just as healthy as fresh, they're available all year and they cut down on waste as they won't linger in the back of your fridge waiting to go off!

SIMPLE SEARED TUNA SALAD

£6.19

I get a lot of my tuna in frozen form from discount supermarkets. It's pretty good quality and if you defrost carefully, it's a really great ingredient to work with. Place the steaks into a kitchen towel and leave for a couple of hours, or overnight if you have the time, to get out as much moisture as possible. This means that when you come to sear them, they sear quickly and don't boil. The size of these steaks is perfect for a starter or light lunch.

SERVES	PREP TIME	COOK TIME		ENERGY (KCALS)	PROTEIN	FAT	SATURATED FAT	CARB.	TOTAL SUGARS	SALT	FIBRE
4	20 MINS	2-3 MINS		364	30	19	3	16	10.5	2	3.5

For the dressing

2 red onions, very finely sliced

1 small bunch of long radishes, very finely sliced

5 tablespoons rice wine vinegar

3 tablespoons mirin

3 tablespoons soy sauce

1 tablespoon very finely chopped fresh ginger

4 tablespoons olive oil

For the salad

100g baby spinach

100g watercress

For the tuna

4 frozen tuna steaks (approx. 100g), defrosted

1 tablespoon any oil

2 tablespoons sesame seeds

salt and freshly ground black pepper

Place all the ingredients for the dressing into a bowl and mix well. Place the spinach and watercress into a separate bowl and mix well.

Pat the tuna steaks dry with a clean tea towel, and then rub over a little oil on both sides. Heat a dry, non-stick frying pan over a high heat. Season the oiled tuna steaks with salt and pepper and add a sprinkling of sesame seeds. Place straight into the hot pan and cook for 1–2 minutes, flip over and cook for a further 1–2 minutes.

While the tuna is cooking, pour the dressing over the watercress and spinach and mix really well. Divide equally between four bowls.

When the tuna is ready, slice each steak into three, lay on the salad and serve.

I came up with this simple salad one warm sunny day when I couldn't be bothered to go shopping for lunch. In the fridge I had radish and chicory left over from a recipe development day, and I had accidently bought microwaveable coconut rice a while ago, so it was languishing in the cupboard. So I put the lot together, seasoned with mirin, soy and rice vinegar and hey presto! I serve this with plain cooked fish such as salmon, mackerel or even grilled fresh herrings.

COCONUT RICE & RADISH SALAD

£5.73

ENERGY (KCALS)	PROTEIN	FAT	SATURATED FAT	CARB.	TOTAL SUGARS	SALT	FIBRE
259	4	12	4.5	34	4	1.3	2

SERVES	PREP TIME	COOK TIME
4	10 MINS	2 MINS

Finely slice the radish and shred the chicory, then place into a bowl. Add the dressing ingredients and mix really well, then add the rice and stir through. Serve warm or at room temperature.

8 plump radishes

1 small head chicory

2 × 250g packets microwaveable coconut rice, warmed for 2 minutes

For the dressing

2 tablespoons extra virgin olive oil

2 tablespoons mirin

4 tablespoons rice wine vinegar

1 tablespoon soy sauce

salt and freshly ground black pepper

TIP

Making the dressing with olive oil and vinegar adds healthy fats to this dish, which improve how well your body absorbs the nutrients from the radishes and chicory.

CARROT, MANGO & PEANUT SALAD

£10.29

I really like the freshness and texture of this salad, and the fact that it encompasses (mostly) raw fruit and vegetables. I use fresh red chilli in this dressing purely for visual impact, but ½ teaspoon dried chilli flakes (my favourite) work equally as well. The canned water chestnuts may seem a little odd, but I like the texture in a finished salad, plus they keep their crunch nicely.

SERVES	PREP TIME
4	15
	MINS

ENERGY (KCALS)	PROTEIN	FAT	SATURATED FAT	CARB.	TOTAL SUGARS	SALT	FIBRE
442	10.5	32.5	5.5	22	18.5	1.4	10

4 medium carrots, cut into very fine strips

5 banana shallots, very thinly sliced

1 green under-ripe mango, cut into very thin strips

225g can water chestnuts, drained then finely sliced

For the dressing

3 tablespoons any oil

4 garlic cloves

½ small red chilli, very finely chopped

1 tablespoon nam pla (optional)

1 tablespoon palm or soft brown sugar, crushed

zest and juice of 4 large limes

salt and freshly ground black pepper

To serve

fresh coriander leaves

fresh Thai basil leaves

100g salted jumbo peanuts, roughly chopped

1 medium ripe avocado, peeled, deseeded, cut into 1cm cubes

Heat a small frying pan over a medium heat and add 1 tablespoon of oil. Finely chop three of the garlic cloves and add to the pan, Fry for a couple of minutes until golden. Crush the remaining garlic clove to a fine paste.

Place the carrots, shallots, mango and water chestnuts into a bowl and mix well.

In a separate bowl, place the chilli, nam pla, if using, fried and crushed garlic, palm or brown sugar, lime juice and zest and the oil and mix really well, then season with salt and pepper. Pour over the raw veg and leave for 30 minutes to soften slightly.

When ready to serve, add the coriander, basil, peanuts and avocado and mix really well. Serve.

TIP

Carrots are well known for their levels of beta carotene (the pigment that gives their colour), which is converted to vitamin A in the body, and peanuts are also packed with goodies such as magnesium, potassium and vitamin E.

GRILLED BREADCRUMB ASPARAGUS

£10.58

I really like to make this dish using the first of the British asparagus; it's a real treat. The mix of textures, taste and colour work really well. You can omit the breadsticks and ham and instead place the asparagus into a baking dish and serve as a starter or main course accompaniment. I sometimes top it with poached eggs, then sprinkle over the crumbs and glaze under a hot grill. It's a really adaptable dish.

SERVES	PREP TIME	COOK TIME
4	20 MINS	20 MINS

ENERGY (KCALS)	PROTEIN	FAT	SATURATED FAT	CARB.	TOTAL SUGARS	SALT	FIBRE
654	18.5	53	5.5	24	6	3.1	3

20 medium asparagus spears, trimmed to the same length, bottom 3cm peeled
4 tablespoons olive oil
10 breadsticks
20 slices air-dried ham
4 tablespoons Dijon mustard
50g Panko breadcrumbs
salt and freshly ground black pepper

For the mayonnaise
200g mayonnaise
50g chopped capers
4 tablespoons chopped fresh basil
zest of 1 lemon

Preheat the grill to medium.

Roll the asparagus in the oil and add a little salt and pepper so that it sticks on nicely. Gently cook the asparagus in a large, non-stick frying pan over a medium heat for 5–6 minutes, depending on their thickness, making sure you have a nice colour all over. Remove from the pan and set aside to cool.

Once the asparagus is cool, cut a breadstick to the same length, or just shorter, as the asparagus spear. Wrap a slice of air-dried ham around the two, nice and tightly. Repeat until all the spears are wrapped.

In the same pan, gently sauté the ham-wrapped asparagus over a medium heat for 4–5 minutes until it takes on a little colour.

Turn over and spread each wrapped spear with a little mustard. Place on a baking tray, then add a sprinkling of breadcrumbs and pop under the grill for 2 minutes to brown slightly.

Meanwhile, stir together the mayonnaise ingredients and season. Serve the grilled asparagus with the caper, basil and lemon mayonnaise.

A colourful and full-flavoured alternative to a bog-standard quiche. There are a couple of things to point out here. Firstly, you part-cook the flan shell and seal with egg to ensure that you have a nice crisp bottom when fully cooked. Secondly, adding a little starch to the mix ensures that all the wet ingredients hold together, as quiche can be a little watery, plus if you slightly overcook the filling, the mix will not split too much. Jarred and canned peppers have great colour and flavour, and there's no faff of roasting and peeling them yourself.

RED PEPPER QUICHE

£12.23

ENERGY (KCALS)	PROTEIN	FAT	SATURATED FAT	CARB.	TOTAL SUGARS	SALT	FIBRE
341	11.5	21	6.5	25	9	1	3.5

SERVES	PREP TIME	COOK TIME
6	30 MINS	35-40 MINS

Preheat the oven to 200°C/gas 6.

Line the flan tin with the pastry, leaving a nice high top edge (you want a really deep finished quiche). Dock well with a fork. Line with greaseproof paper and fill to the top with baking beans. Place the case onto a baking tray and bake for 20 minutes to set the pastry.

Heat the olive oil in a sauté pan over a low heat. Add the peppers to the pan. Reduce the heat and cover with a tight-fitting lid, then cook for 20 minutes until really soft. (It's essential that you keep the lid on to prevent the juices from evaporating.) Remove from the heat and set aside to cool.

Carefully remove the beans and paper from the base and brush with the beaten egg. Return to the oven for 2 minutes to set the egg.

Place the cooled peppers with all their oil and juices into a blender. Add the garlic, stock cube and some ground pepper, then blitz until you have a smooth purée. Add the milk, remaining eggs, the egg yolks and the cornflour or arrowroot, and pulse to blend again.

Pour three-quarters of the pepper custard into the flan, then place on a tray in the oven (just in case you get a leak or run over slightly). With the door open, fill the flan right to the brim with the rest of the custard. Cook for 25 minutes, or until just wobbly in the centre: do not overcook or the quiche will soufflé and split.

Remove from the oven, then leave to cool for at least 30 minutes. Serve at room temperature with a dressed green salad.

225g sheet ready rolled shortcrust pastry, rolled to fit a 23cm-round, 4cm-deep loose-bottomed flan tin

2 tablespoons extra virgin olive oil

4 canned, deseeded red peppers (800g flesh), chopped

3 medium eggs, 1 beaten

4 garlic cloves, finely chopped

10g reduced-salt vegetable stock cube

568ml skimmed milk

2 medium egg yolks

2 tablespoons cornflour or arrowroot powder

freshly ground black pepper

WEEKNIGHT SUPPERS

Now, this is a cooking technique I stumbled upon quite by accident. Normally I griddle, pan-fry, bake or microwave – or even remove the ears with a sharp knife and sauté – and the end result is fine. This method slices the corn lengthways (yes, it's a bit fiddly and you need a sharp knife but it makes them so much easier to eat), so you end up with four long quarters. You then fry the quarters ear-side down. If you're serving them as a side, for example with burgers (see pages 87 and 88), they look far nicer than normal sweetcorn.

CURLY SWEETCORN

£3.00

ENERGY (KCALS)	PROTEIN	FAT	SATURATED FAT	CARB.	TOTAL SUGARS	SALT	FIBRE
114	3.5	7.5	0.6	8	2	0.5	2

SERVES	PREP TIME	COOK TIME
4	15	15
AS A SIDE	MINS	MINS

Preheat the oven to 220°C/gas 7.

Using a very sharp knife, carefully cut the sweetcorn lengthways down the centre of each husk, then cut in half lengthways again, making four long pieces. Season the corn well with salt and pepper.

Heat some oil in a large frying pan over a medium heat. Place the corn into the warm oil, ear-side down. Gently sauté for a few minutes until it takes on a little colour, turning occasionally.

Pop the whole pan into the oven and cook for 5–6 minutes. Once cooked, remove from the oven and set aside the corn to cool for 5 minutes.

To eat, pick up and bend the corn; it makes them so much easier to eat.

4 large, fresh sweetcorn cobs
vegetable oil
salt and freshly ground black
    pepper

For this dish to taste really good, the mushrooms have to be really well cooked and dry to increase their flavour. To do this you cook longer than you normally would, until the pan is very dry. I also add yeast extract, such as Marmite, or some Bovril; even this tiny amount really deepens the flavour of the mushrooms and asparagus.

ASPARAGUS & GARLIC MUSHROOMS

£5.41

ENERGY (KCALS)	PROTEIN	FAT	SATURATED FAT	CARB.	TOTAL SUGARS	SALT	FIBRE
166	6	12	2	6.5	5.5	0.1	4.5

SERVES	PREP TIME	COOK TIME
4	25 MINS	20 MINS

Heat half the oil in a wok or large frying pan over a medium heat. Add the onions and garlic, and stir to slightly soften. Add the mushrooms and cook for a good 15 minutes to release all their water, or until they are very dry.

Remove the mushrooms, onions and garlic from the pan from the pan, and wipe out with a little kitchen paper. Place it over a high heat and add the remaining oil. Add the asparagus and season well with salt and pepper, then cook for 5–6 minutes until they take on a little colour.

Add the mushroom mixture back into the pan and add a dash of hot sauce, if using, or yeast extract (or both) and season again. Warm through and serve.

4 tablespoons extra virgin olive oil

3 small onions, finely chopped

2 garlic cloves, finely crushed to a paste

250g brown cap mushrooms

500g trimmed asparagus, cut into 2cm pieces

Sriracha sauce (optional)

½ teaspoon yeast extract (optional)

salt and freshly ground black pepper

TIP

Low in fat (and calories) and packed with vitamins, asparagus is also a great source of fibre and can help with digestion – so less bloat! It also contains vitamins E (strengthens your immune system) and K (keeps bones healthy).

POTATO NACHOS WITH SALSA

£9.80

A twist on the classic Tex-Mex style offering. Here I bake potato slices rather than using fried tortilla chips and half cook a salsa to increase its depth of flavour. Crème fraîche or soured cream is an optional extra; you can use 0 per cent fat yogurt instead if you so wish.

SERVES	PREP TIME	COOK TIME		ENERGY (KCALS)	PROTEIN	FAT	SATURATED FAT	CARB.	TOTAL SUGARS	SALT	FIBRE
4	35-40 MINS	35-40 MINS		1146	12	89	18	68	11	2.6	13

For the potatoes

6 medium red-skinned potatoes, washed well

1½ tablespoons olive oil

salt and freshly ground pepper

For the salsa

3 tablespoons extra virgin olive oil

2 small red onions, very finely chopped

2 garlic cloves, crushed to a paste

2 tablespoons tomato purée

400g sun-dried tomatoes, chopped

2 ripe plum tomatoes, roughly chopped

4 tablespoons roughly chopped fresh coriander, plus extra whole leaves to serve

juice of 2 large limes

2-3 tablespoons sherry vinegar

To serve

2 ripe avocados, peeled, deseeded and chopped

100ml reduced-fat crème fraîche or soured cream (optional)

fresh chives, roughly chopped

Preheat the oven to 220°C/gas 7.

Slice the potatoes 5mm thick, leaving the skin on, then place into a bowl. Add the olive oil and some salt and pepper and mix well. Lay the slices on baking sheets and bake for 20 minutes until cooked and slightly crispy on the edges.

Meanwhile for the salsa, heat the olive oil in a frying pan over a medium heat, then add the onions and garlic and soften for 2–3 minutes. Add the tomato purée and cook for a further 2–3 minutes. Add the sun-dried tomatoes, mix well and then remove from the heat and set aside to cool.

Once cool, add the chopped plum tomatoes, coriander, lime juice and sherry vinegar, and season well with salt and pepper.

Once the potatoes are cooked, remove from the oven and arrange on plates. Spoon over the salsa, avocado and crème fraîche or soured cream. Sprinkle over some coriander leaves and roughly chopped chives.

I cooked this dish on the Lyme bay beach on the longest day of 2018. All I had was a large, open fire pit and two large sauté pans. The freshness of the fish made this dish. I love gurnard, though bass, mackerel and whiting work equally as well. Just remember not to overcook the fish.

GURNARD, COURGETTES & TOMATOES

£13.00

ENERGY (KCALS)	PROTEIN	FAT	SATURATED FAT	CARB.	TOTAL SUGARS	SALT	FIBRE
406	39	18.5	3	19	7	0.7	3.5

SERVES	PREP TIME	COOK TIME
4	20 MINS	20 MINS

Heat the 4 tablespoons of oil in a frying pan over a medium heat. Add the onions and fry for 5–6 minutes to soften, then add the garlic and oregano and fry for 1–2 minutes: do not overcook. Add the courgettes and gently sauté for a further 5–6 minutes.

Add the tomatoes, paprika, vinegar, some salt and pepper and a dash of water, and cook over a medium heat for 5–6 minutes, or until the tomatoes soften and some of the moisture is cooked off.

Remove from the heat, then add the basil and stir, so the basil just warms through.

Season the gurnard fillets and dust with a little flour. Heat the 2 tablespoons of oil in a frying pan over a low heat. Gently fry the fillets in the oil for 3–4 minutes, then turn over and fry on the other side for a further 2–3 minutes. Remove from the heat and leave to rest for roughly 8 minutes.

To serve, season the tomatoes and courgette again, spoon half onto four plates, top with the fish and top with the rest of the tomatoes and courgettes. Sprinkle over a little more fresh basil and serve.

4 tablespoons olive oil

2 small red onions, finely chopped

2 garlic cloves

2 teaspoons dried oregano

2 medium courgettes,
    cut into 5mm pieces

4–6 ripe medium tomatoes,
    roughly chopped

pinch of smoked paprika

2 tablespoons any vinegar

4 tablespoons roughly chopped
    fresh basil, plus extra to serve

salt and freshly ground
    black pepper

For the fish

800g filleted gurnard (or bass,
    mackerel or whiting), skin-on but
    scaled, cut into 4cm slices

2 tablespoons flour

2 tablespoons olive oil

TIP

High in protein and low in fat, gurnard is a healthy and sustainable fish that is also calcium and potassium-rich; all essential for packing in the minerals and curbing your hunger.

I love simplicity, and this dish is a perfect example of how simple cooking can be a real winner. You have not only your five vegetables for the day but also a small amount of protein, bulked out by the veg. Personally, I leave the skin on, but you can remove if you want to reduce more calories, or just want a lower-fat dish.

ROASTED CHICKEN TRAY BAKE

£5.33

ENERGY (KCALS)	PROTEIN	FAT	SATURATED FAT	CARB.	TOTAL SUGARS	SALT	FIBRE
615	40	20	4	61	19	0.7	14

SERVES	PREP TIME	COOK TIME
4	15 MINS	50-70 MINS

Preheat the oven to 200°C/gas 6.

Mix the potatoes and all the vegetables together in a bowl, then add the olive oil and some salt and pepper and mix well. Spread evenly in a baking tray, then pop in the oven to heat through while you brown the chicken.

Season the chicken thighs, then heat a non-stick frying pan over a high heat. Add the seasoned chicken thighs, skin-side down, and fry for 2–3 minutes until they take on a little colour.

Transfer the thighs to the vegetable tray in the oven and cook for 45 minutes to 1 hour, or until the chicken is cooked through and all the vegetables are nicely cooked. Serve.

3 large potatoes, peeled and cut into 1cm pieces

1 small butternut squash, peeled and cut into 1cm pieces

2 large carrots, peeled and cut into 1cm pieces

2 red onions, sliced

2 large leeks, cut into 4cm pieces

4 tablespoons olive oil

8 small chicken thighs, bone in

salt and freshly ground black pepper

SMOKED TURKEY THAI WRAPS

£4.16

I like wraps, but the filling has to be really tasty and packed full of great textures. Here, I've used wafer-thin or shaved turkey, so you only need 50 grams per person. I have also added big flavours like fish sauce, chilli and lime to add a kick to the filling. Cabbage, tomatoes and lots of coriander finish the wrap off perfectly – and there's no added salt.

SERVES	PREP TIME
4	15
WRAPS	MINS

ENERGY (KCALS)	PROTEIN	FAT	SATURATED FAT	CARB.	TOTAL SUGARS	SALT	FIBRE
513	27	15	3.5	64.5	9	2.8	5

1 medium carrots, finely shredded

200g wafer-thin smoked turkey

1 teaspoon chopped fresh red chilli

4 tablespoons freshly
    chopped coriander

2 tablespoons chopped
    unsalted cashews

a small handful of finely sliced
    white cabbage

8 cherry tomatoes, halved

2 tablespoons Thai fish sauce

3 tablespoons lime juice

2 tablespoons olive oil

2 teaspoons sugar

4 large wheat tortillas

freshly ground black pepper

Mix together the carrots, turkey, chilli, coriander, cashews, cabbage and tomatoes. Add the fish sauce, lime juice, olive oil, sugar and some pepper, then mix really well.

Place a quarter of the filling at the edge of one tortilla. Fold the bottom over to just cover the filling. Fold the sides in and, at the same time, roll up from the bottom until the wrap is tight and fully rolled. Wrap tightly in greaseproof paper and slice on a long angle.

TIP

Using smoked turkey means you get extra flavour for less weight, so you can save calories (and cash) by using only a small amount of turkey cut wafer-thin.

Leg or brown meat on turkey makes better burgers because the meat is juicier. I don't want to get too techy, but it's to do with the leg muscles working harder, which applies to all white leg meat (even game). Breast meat is fine, and is extremely good for you, but needs more attention. Skinned turkey breast can be less than 2 per cent fat, so it can cook dry with a crumbly texture. I have a couple of great tricks to avoid this: add a little mayonnaise to keep the burger beautifully juicy and tasty; and dust with a little cornflour to trap the juice in the burger.

JUICY TURKEY BURGERS

£4.14

ENERGY (KCALS)	PROTEIN	FAT	SATURATED FAT	CARB.	TOTAL SUGARS	SALT	FIBRE
247	25	7.5	1.5	20	2.5	0.9	0.1

SERVES	PREP TIME	COOK TIME	CHILL TIME
4	20 MINS	10-12 MINS	30 MINS

Place the turkey, mayonnaise, basil, Worcestershire sauce and egg white into a bowl. Mix really well, then add the seasoning and breadcrumbs and mix well again. Leave to chill in the fridge for 30 minutes, for the mixture to tighten once the breadcrumbs reconstitute themselves.

Mould the mixture into four balls, then flatten nice and thinly into small patties, and chill for a further 15 minutes.

To cook, lightly spray a non-stick pan over a medium heat with a little olive oil. Dust the patties with a little cornflour and cook for 2–3 minutes. Turn over and cook for a further 3–4 minutes.

400g minced turkey
  (preferably leg meat)
1 tablespoon mayonnaise
4 tablespoons roughly
  chopped basil
2 tablespoons Worcestershire sauce
1 medium egg white, lightly beaten
4–5 tablespoons dried
  breadcrumbs
olive oil (in a spray bottle)
2 tablespoons cornflour
salt
ground white pepper

BURGERS & CHIPS

£5.30

Burger and chips had to be on my list. Yes, we can buy them everywhere, but sometimes it's quite nice to make them yourself. Here I bake sweet potatoes in the oven, reduce the beef element to 100 grams per person and don't add salt. The key is to ensure you mix the mince really well so you get a patty texture, or the burger will be dry and crumbly. Oh, and I detest the new craze for sweet brioche-style buns with burgers: sesame is the only way!

SERVES	PREP TIME	CHILL TIME	COOK TIME
4	20 MINS	45 MINS	40 MINS

ENERGY (KCALS)	PROTEIN	FAT	SATURATED FAT	CARB.	TOTAL SUGARS	SALT	FIBRE
753	36	23	8	97	26	3.7	8.5

For the chips

600g sweet potato, washed well
   and cut into little finger-thick
   slices (skin on)
1 tablespoon cornflour,
   arrowroot powder or
   tapioca starch
freshly ground black pepper

For the burgers

400g 12% fat minced beef
1 onion, very finely chopped
2 tablespoons Worcestershire sauce
1 medium egg white, beaten
4–5 tablespoons breadcrumbs,
   made from leftover stale bread
vegetable oil (in a spray bottle)
4 slices individually wrapped
   burger cheese
4 sesame burger buns
1 large beef tomato, sliced into 4
4 crisp salad leaves
2 gherkins sliced into 8
8 teaspoons ketchup
4 teaspoons mustard
ground white pepper

Cut the sweet potatoes into chips, then soak in cold water for 1 hour.

Preheat the oven to 200°C/gas 6.

Place the beef, onion, Worcestershire sauce, egg white and some white pepper into a bowl. Mix really well, then add the breadcrumbs and mix well again. Leave to chill in the fridge for 30 minutes, so the mixture can tighten, once the breadcrumbs reconstitute themselves.

Mould into four balls, flatten nice and thinly into large patties, then chill again for 15 minutes.

Once the potatoes are soaked, drain, dry with a clean kitchen towel and dust with the cornflour, arrowroot or tapioca starch, then season. Bake in the oven for 20–25 minutes, or until crispy and well coloured.

To cook the burgers, lightly spray a non-stick lidded frying pan with two bursts of oil. Cook the burgers for 2–3 minutes, flip over and place one slice of cheese on each burger, then cover and cook for a further 1–2 minutes to cook the burger and melt the cheese.

Assemble the burgers with half the bun on the bottom, then tomato, lettuce, burger, gherkin, ketchup and mustard, and then top with the other half of the bun.

Sweet potato may have more sugar than white potato, but it contains fewer carbs and calories overall, plus it is a great source of vitamins. Baking the chips in the oven instead of deep-frying them means they don't absorb as much fat, so they're healthier all round.

Get the kids involved making their own pizza with this really easy recipe. I don't use yeast for the raising of the dough but good, old-fashioned self-raising flour. If you are using pepperoni you can get away with four very thin slices on each pizza. For a lower fat, meaty alternative topping, use wafer-thin ham or some leftover chicken marinated in paprika and pepper. These both freeze well and can be baked off when needed.

PIZZA

£7.07

ENERGY (KCALS)	PROTEIN	FAT	SATURATED FAT	CARB.	TOTAL SUGARS	SALT	FIBRE	SERVES	PREP TIME	COOK TIME
474	28.5	19	8	44	6.5	0.6	7	8	20 MINS	25–40 MINS

Preheat the oven to 220°C/gas 7.

Heat the oil in a saucepan over a high heat. Add the onion and cook for 2–3 minutes until it takes on a little colour. Add the garlic and cook for a further 2 minutes, but do not burn. Add the tomatoes, purée and vinegar and cook down until you have a thick, dry pulp, about 15 minutes.

Place the flour, salt, basil, oregano and some pepper into a bowl and mix well. Add the yogurt and enough water to make a soft dough (it shouldn't look too dry or too wet). Knead, but don't over knead, then cut into eight. Roll out each of the balls on a lightly floured surface nice and thin until about 16–18cm in diameter.

Place the pizza bases onto baking sheets lined with greaseproof paper and dock with a fork. (If you wish, you may freeze the dough at this point.) Bake in the oven for 10 minutes to set the base, then remove.

Spoon over the tomato sauce thinly and evenly, close to the edge. Break the mozzarella into small lumps and dot over evenly, then add the pepperoni, if using. Add the basil leaves, drizzle over the olive oil and season with pepper. Return to the oven and bake until cooked and crisp, about 8 minutes. Serve.

For the sauce
30ml extra virgin olive oil
1 medium onion, finely chopped
2 garlic cloves, finely chopped
400g can chopped tomatoes
2 tablespoons tomato purée
1 tablespoon any vinegar (I use
   malt vinegar)

For the base
450g self-raising wholemeal flour,
   plus extra for dusting
pinch of salt
4 tablespoons chopped fresh basil
2 teaspoons dried oregano
200g 0% fat yogurt
freshly ground black pepper

For the toppings
750g reduced-fat mozzarella
2 bunches of fresh basil
50ml olive oil
120g pepperoni (optional)

TIP

I use low-fat versions of yogurt and mozzarella to save on the calories without sacrificing on flavour. Plus, using wholemeal flour instead of white is better for you in fibre content.

I often use jarred peppers, as they are great value for money and really good quality. Having said that, I do like freshly roasted, peeled peppers, but preparing them can be a bit of work, though it's great if you have the time. Canned tomatoes are a real life-saver if you want to make a quick, easy sauce for meat, fish or vegan dishes. Here I use cooked prawns, but the freshwater variety (fresh or frozen) work equally as well. I frequently use dried chilli flakes purely to better gauge exactly how much heat I'm adding: there's a huge array of fresh chillies now and some can blow your socks off.

SPICY PRAWN & BASIL TAGLIERINI

£10.55

ENERGY (KCALS)	PROTEIN	FAT	SATURATED FAT	CARB.	TOTAL SUGARS	SALT	FIBRE
515	27	14	2	68	13	2.2	7

SERVES	PREP TIME	COOK TIME
4	20 MINS	20 MINS

In a large pan, heat the oil over a medium heat and add the onion, garlic and chilli, then fry for 5–6 minutes.

Meanwhile, put the peppers and stock cube into a blender and blend. Pour into the cooking onions, garlic and chilli along with the tomatoes.

Add the spinach, heat through to wilt and then simmer for 5–6 minutes to thicken slightly. Just before serving add the prawns and warm for 4 minutes, then add the pasta and basil and stir though.

4 tablespoons olive oil

2 large onion, finely chopped

4 garlic cloves

½ teaspoon dried chilli flakes

380g jar roasted peppers in oil, drained

10g vegetable stock cube

400g chopped tomatoes

150g spinach

300g Atlantic cooked prawns, roughly chopped

300g taglierini, cooked with a dash of oil to stop sticking together

2 tablespoons chopped fresh basil

salt and freshly ground black pepper

NATION'S FAVOURITE DISH

SPAGHETTI BOLOGNESE

£3.76

A little sauce goes a long way here, so I've halved the meat content but added more vegetables to compensate for the bulk loss. The sauce will coat the spaghetti perfectly, saving you money and calories. You can add a little finely grated Parmesan cheese, if you like, at the end. I use a microplane grater, which makes 20 grams look and go a long way!

SERVES	PREP TIME	COOK TIME
4	20 MINS	30-35 MINS

ENERGY (KCALS)	PROTEIN	FAT	SATURATED FAT	CARB.	TOTAL SUGARS	SALT	FIBRE
615	32	19	5	75	14	0.9	9.5

1 tablespoon extra virgin olive oil (or a couple of squirts from a spray bottle)

2 small onions, very finely chopped

4 small celery sticks, very finely chopped

2 large carrots, peeled and very finely chopped

4 garlic cloves, finely chopped

1 teaspoon dried oregano

400g 12% fat minced beef

2 tablespoons flour

2 tablespoons tomato purée

400g can chopped tomatoes

½ × 10g any stock cube

300g dried spaghetti

freshly ground black pepper

Heat the olive oil in a large pan over a medium heat and add the onions, celery, carrots, garlic and oregano. Cook for 10 minutes to soften.

Add the mince and break up with a wooden spoon, then cook for about 5 minutes. Add the flour to soak up the juices, and stir really well to coat. Add the tomato purée and chopped tomatoes, then using the can, refill with water and add to the pan. Stir well.

Add a little pepper and the stock cube, stir, bring the pan to the boil, then simmer for 15 minutes, or until the vegetables are cooked and the sauce thickened nicely.

Meanwhile, cook the spaghetti according to the packet instructions. When everything is ready, add the cooked spaghetti to the sauce and mix well. Serve.

TIP

Using a strong cheese like Parmesan means you get lots of flavour for relatively few calories and a low cost. And swapping the meat for more veg means less saturated fat.

Swapping half the meat for lentils not only reduces this classic's saturated fat content, but also adds heart-healthy potassium and folic acid. Lentils are also filling thanks to their high fibre content, so the smaller portion size goes a long way.

A true classic here, but with reduced calories and salt, plus a smaller portion size. Removing half the meat protein and adding cooked lentils is a great trick and really works well. A good tip here is to use a smaller but deeper baking dish, so you will end up with a deeper end result. This dish can be made in advance and frozen, then defrosted and cooked at a later time. If you take that route, then make the meat sauce slightly wetter to allow for absorption by the raw pasta sheets.

LASAGNE

£4.18

ENERGY (KCALS)	PROTEIN	FAT	SATURATED FAT	CARB.	TOTAL SUGARS	SALT	FIBRE
594	32	22	8	63	11	1.5	7

SERVES	PREP TIME	COOK TIME
4	25 MINS	1-1.5 HRS

Heat the oil in a frying pan over a medium heat and add the onions. Sauté for 15 minutes, then add the garlic and cook for a further 2 minutes. Add the mince and cook for 6–8 minutes until lightly coloured, breaking up with a spatula. Add the lentils, tomatoes, stock cube, 200ml of water and the herbs and season with salt, if using, and pepper. Bring to the boil and simmer for 20–25 minutes, taking care to watch it as it may catch slightly.

Meanwhile, make the white sauce. Heat the milk in a small pan. Mix the butter and flour together well, then whisk this mixture into the simmering milk: it will thicken almost immediately. Add salt and pepper, then remove from the heat and keep warm.

Heat the oven to 190°C/gas 5.

Spoon a little of the meat sauce into a 25cm square baking dish. Place three lasagne sheets over the top to cover well. Add a layer of half the white sauce, then add another layer of the remaining meat sauce. Add a second layer of pasta and finally top with the remaining white sauce. (If you are freezing the dish in advance, freeze at this point.) Sprinkle over the cheese, if using, and bake in the oven for 35–45 minutes. Remove from the oven and cool slightly before eating with a large green salad.

300g (6) dried lasagne sheets
20g Parmesan, grated (optional)

For the meat sauce
2 tablespoons olive oil
2 small onions, finely chopped
4 garlic cloves, chopped
250g 12% fat minced beef
400g can green lentils (drained weight 265g)
400g can chopped tomatoes
½ × 10g reduced-salt beef or chicken stock cube
1 tablespoon dried oregano
4 tablespoons roughly chopped fresh basil
salt (optional)
freshly ground black pepper

For the white sauce
300ml skimmed milk
20g flour
20g soft butter

I really like this recipe: not only is it packed full of flavour and texture, but also it is a really hearty meal for four people. I sometimes stretch it to serve six. I like adding frozen veg; they are really good value for money and always available. Plus I love, love frozen mash! Let the purists sneer.

NATION'S FAVOURITE DISH

COTTAGE PIE

£6.02

ENERGY (KCALS)	PROTEIN	FAT	SATURATED FAT	CARB.	TOTAL SUGARS	SALT	FIBRE
468	26	18	7.5	46	12	2.2	9

SERVES	PREP TIME	COOK TIME
4	20 MINS	1-1.5 HRS

Heat the oil in a frying pan over a medium heat and add the mushrooms. Fry for 15 minutes until the moisture from the mushrooms begins to reduce. Add the onions and mince and break up well.

Fry for 15 minutes until all the moisture has evaporated and the mince starts to brown in the oil and its fat. Add the flour and mix well, then cook for a further 2–3 minutes, or until the flour browns well on the bottom of the pan.

Add the tomato purée, thyme, Worcestershire sauce, yeast extract, stock cube and enough water to just cover the meat (about 300ml). Season well with pepper and check the salt – as there is already salt in the stock cube you probably won't need it. Lower the heat and cook gently for 20–25 minutes, stirring occasionally so the flour doesn't catch.

Add the vegetables and wilt in the spinach, mixing well: it should be fairly thick. Spoon into a baking dish and leave to cool.

Place the butterbeans into a bowl and break up with a potato masher, then add the defrosted mash and mix well. Add a little milk and season with pepper and salt, if needed: the mash should be soft but not too creamy. Spoon onto the cooled, set mince and fluff up with a fork.

When ready, preheat the oven to 200°C/gas 6, then bake for 20–25 minutes until golden and slightly crunchy.

1 tablespoon any oil
250g chestnut mushrooms, very finely chopped (I use a Magimix)
4 small onions, finely chopped
250g 12% fat beef mince
2–3 tablespoons plain flour
2 tablespoons tomato purée
pinch of dried thyme
2 tablespoons Worcestershire sauce
2 teaspoons yeast extract
½ × 10g reduced-salt stock cube
250g frozen mixed vegetables
250g fresh spinach
400g can butter beans
400g frozen mash pellets, defrosted
150ml hot skimmed milk
salt (optional)
freshly ground black pepper

VEGETABLE SHEPHERD'S PIE

£3.83

The recipe title may sound like a bit of an oxymoron, but you know what I mean. This is quite a nice alternative to a meat version, and it's nice to bring some changes to the potato topping. I add yeast extract instead of Worcestershire sauce; you could also add a little brown miso paste to help develop the flavour profile if you like, though take care as it can be quite salty.

SERVES	PREP TIME	COOK TIME
4	20 MINS	1.5-2 HRS

ENERGY (KCALS)	PROTEIN	FAT	SATURATED FAT	CARB.	TOTAL SUGARS	SALT	FIBRE
630	23	26	9	70	17	3.3	14.5

4 tablespoons any oil

400g chestnut mushrooms, very finely chopped (I use a Magimix)

4 small onions, finely chopped

2 × 400g cans or packets cooked green lentils, well drained

2-3 tablespoons plain flour

2 tablespoons tomato purée

pinch of dried thyme

2 tablespoons yeast extract (such as Marmite) or vegetable Bovril

2 × 10g vegetable stock cube

salt and freshly ground black pepper

For the mash

350g potatoes

350g sweet potatoes

1 small cauliflower, chopped into small chunks

150ml hot milk

50g butter or olive oil

Heat the oil in a frying pan over a medium heat and add the mushrooms. Cook for 15 minutes to reduce the moisture. Add the onions and lentils and break up well. Cook for 15 minutes until all the moisture has evaporated.

Add the flour and mix well, then cook for a further 2–3 minutes until the flour browns well on the bottom of the pan. Next add the tomato purée, thyme, yeast extract, stock cubes and enough water to just cover the vegetables. Season well with pepper (check the salt – you may not need it) and cook for 20–25 minutes – gently or the flour will catch – stirring occasionally. After this time, the mixture should be fairly thick: pour or spoon into a baking dish and leave to cool.

Preheat the oven to 190°C/gas 5.

Gently boil both types of potato together for 15–20 minutes. Once cooked, add the cauliflower and cook for a further 10 minutes, then drain well. Mash everything really well together, then whisk the hot milk and butter or oil into the mash and season well with salt and pepper. The mash should be not too creamy but soft.

Spoon onto the cooled, set mince and fluff up with a fork. When ready, heat in the oven for 20–25 minutes until golden and slightly crunchy. Serve with microwaved wedges of spring greens and peas.

MIXED VEGETABLE HOTPOT

£6.18

SERVES	PREP TIME	COOK TIME
4	35	1.5
	MINS	HRS

This hearty dish works really well and is a real tummy warmer. I add jackfruit as the 'meat' element, however it can be a bit pricey, so you can use Quorn or tofu instead. At first I wasn't a fan of jackfruit but it's grown on me. The problem was that chefs and writers were adding so many flavourings like salt, sugar, oil, fat, etc. to give it some flavour, that it became counterproductive to use it as a healthy alternative to meat or fish protein. Here, it's used with vegetables, pulses and grains to develop the depth of flavour while also being extremely good for you.

ENERGY (KCALS)	PROTEIN	FAT	SATURATED FAT	CARB.	TOTAL SUGARS	SALT	FIBRE
742	20	26	3.5	98	24	2.4	16

8–10 tablespoons any oil

1 large carrot, peeled and chopped

2 onions, chopped

2 celery sticks, finely chopped

2 garlic cloves, crushed

4 tablespoons flour

400g can chickpeas, drained

400g can borlotti beans, drained

400g can chopped tomatoes

3 tablespoons short-grain rice or pearl barley

300g can jackfruit, drained

3 large portobello mushrooms, sliced horizontally into thirds

2 × 10g mushroom or vegetable stock cubes

4 large baking potatoes, peeled and sliced 5mm thin

500ml boiling water

salt and freshly ground black pepper

Preheat the oven to 190°C/gas 5.

Heat 4 tablespoons of the oil in a frying pan over a medium heat and lightly brown the carrots, onions, celery and garlic for 10 minutes. Add the flour and mix through well, then season with a little salt and pepper. Add the chickpeas, beans, tomatoes and rice or barley and mix well, then pour into a roughly 30 × 35cm, 6cm-deep baking dish.

Place the jackfruit evenly over the bean mixture, and press down slightly. Lay over the large mushroom slices, slightly overlapping, and press down. Crumble over the stock cubes, and press down again. Overlap the sliced potatoes over the whole dish and press slightly.

Pour in the boiling water until it comes just halfway up the potatoes but doesn't cover them. Season the potatoes well with salt and pepper, then brush with a little oil. Place the dish on a baking tray, cover with foil and bake in the oven for 45–50 minutes, or until the potatoes are just cooked.

Carefully remove the dish from the oven, then remove the foil and gently press down the potatoes with a potato masher. Increase the oven temperature to 220°C/gas 7. Brush the potatoes with a little more oil and place the dish back in the oven for a further 25–30 minutes to brown nicely and reduce the stock.

Leave to cool for 20 minutes before serving; this dish is even better the next day, warmed gently in a moderate oven or in a microwave.

I love chow mein, especially the Singapore version with curry spices and chilli. Here I've tried to add as many textures and flavours as possible, while cutting down on the overall protein, salt and fat content. You can pack it out further with more vegetables if you prefer and omit any meat protein altogether. I cook this in two batches and then mix them both together; it also freezes well.

CHOW MEIN

£4.74

ENERGY (KCALS)	PROTEIN	FAT	SATURATED FAT	CARB.	TOTAL SUGARS	SALT	FIBRE
329	25	9	1.5	34	11	2.8	7

SERVES	PREP TIME	COOK TIME
4	20 MINS	15 MINS

Heat half the oil in a wok over a high heat, and then add half the spring onions, ginger, garlic and peppers. Stir-fry for 2 minutes, or until they take on a little colour.

Add half the meat, beansprouts and mange tout and stir-fry for a couple of minutes. Next add half the ketchup, oyster sauce and soy sauce with a touch of water. Heat through for a few minutes, then finally add half the noodles and stir through.

Repeat with the remaining ingredients, then mix together the two batches.

2 tablespoons any oil

6 spring onions, sliced on a long diagonal

50g fresh ginger, peeled and cut into fine strips

4 garlic cloves, finely chopped

1 red pepper

1 yellow pepper

1 green pepper

200g cooked chicken, pork or turkey

400g beansprouts

100g mange tout, sliced (or frozen green beans)

4 tablespoons reduced-sugar ketchup

4 tablespoons oyster sauce (optional)

2 tablespoons reduced-salt soy sauce

2 egg noodle nests (or rice or wholemeal noodles), cooked

TIP

To cut cost, you can use frozen green beans instead of the mange tout, and use up any cooked leftover meat – there's no need to buy fresh or precooked meat.

Instead of using all rice, in this recipe cauliflower is ground up to resemble grains. I have to say I was pleasantly surprised how this dish turned out: I was quite sceptical about removing pretty much half the main component of the dish. However, in the end the cauliflower really made up for the loss of rice. I'll point out that you need to cook the cauliflower for a few minutes to drive off some of the moisture, or the end result can be a little bland. Plus, despite removing the egg yolks from the omelette, you will never notice the difference once it's stirred into the finished dish.

SPECIAL-FRIED RICE

£3.43

ENERGY (KCALS)	PROTEIN	FAT	SATURATED FAT	CARB.	TOTAL SUGARS	SALT	FIBRE
269	17	11	2	23	5	1.7	4

SERVES	PREP TIME	COOK TIME
4	20 MINS	15 MINS

Mix the egg yolks and whites together with 2 tablespoons of the soy sauce and a dash of pepper. Heat 1 tablespoon of the oil in a frying pan over a medium heat, then add the eggs and spread out evenly. Gently draw the edges of the cooked egg from the sides of the pan so you end up with a nice, flat omelette. Once fully cooked (about 3–4 minutes), pop the omelette onto a plate

In a large, non-stick wok, heat the remaining tablespoon of oil over a high heat. Fry the garlic, chilli and spring onions for 1–2 minutes, then add the cauliflower rice and stir well. Cook for 3–4 minutes, stirring well to release some of its moisture.

Add the brown rice, Chinese 5 spice and the remaining 2 tablespoons of soy sauce. Add the defrosted vegetables to the wok and stir-fry for a further 2–3 minutes

Add the prawns, ham and chicken and cook for 3–4 minutes to warm through, ensuring they are properly reheated.

Finally, slice the omelette and mix into the pan. Serve.

2 egg yolks
4 egg whites
4 tablespoons reduced-salt soy sauce
2 tablespoons vegetable oil
2 garlic cloves, chopped
1 small red chilli, finely chopped
4 spring onions, sliced on a diagonal
200g cauliflower (1 small whole), finely processed in a food-processor to 'cauliflower rice' consistency
200g cooked brown rice
1 teaspoon Chinese 5 spice
200g mixed frozen vegetables, defrosted
70g cooked cold-water prawns
30g wafer-thin ham
50g leftover or cooked chicken
freshly ground black pepper

TIP

Cauliflower is a high-fibre, low-carb alternative to rice, which drastically cuts the calories of this favourite dish. If you don't have a food-processor, you can chop or shave finely with a sharp knife instead.

SMOKED TOFU STIR-FRY

£9.75

I use a lot of grains in my cooking and find that they bring a lovely texture to any dish. The only thing you have to remember is to soak them overnight in plenty of cold water; if you don't, they can take an age to cook. As with any stir-fry, I always blanch my onions and peppers, which just takes out a little harshness from the dish and makes it far nicer to eat. I like all forms of tofu, especially the slightly firmer and smoked offering.

SERVES	PREP TIME	SOAK TIME	COOK TIME
4	35 MINS	12 HRS	45-50 MINS

ENERGY (KCALS)	PROTEIN	FAT	SATURATED FAT	CARB.	TOTAL SUGARS	SALT	FIBRE
481	28	14	2	53	27	0.16	13

200g kamut, soaked overnight

175g barley, soaked overnight

2 medium onions, very finely sliced

1 red pepper, very finely sliced

1 yellow pepper very finely sliced

1 green pepper, very finely sliced

4 tablespoons any oil

pinch of 5 spice

2 tablespoons soy sauce

450g smoked tofu, cut into
    1cm cubes

1 tablespoon brown miso paste,
    mixed with 2 tablespoons water

200g baby spinach

Place the kamut and barley into a saucepan and cover with cold water. Bring to the boil and then simmer for 35–45 minutes, or until soft and nicely cooked through, then drain.

Meanwhile, in a separate pan place the onions and peppers and cover with cold water. Bring to the boil and then immediately strain in a colander.

Heat the oil in a large wok or frying pan over a high heat, then add the onions, peppers and 5 spice. Cook for 5–6 minutes to get a nice colour. Add the tofu and brown slightly for 3–4 minutes. Add the kamut and barley, soy sauce and miso and cook for 5 minutes or so to bring everything together.

Finally, add the spinach and quickly wilt. Check the seasoning and serve.

TIP

An ancient grain and type of wheat, kamut contains more protein than many other grains. Both kamut and barley are high in fibre, which are essential for healthy digestion and can help lower cholesterol.

CROWD
PLEASERS

FISH & CHIPS

£6.08

In this recipe, I use a 100g fillet of skinned, boneless frozen pollock per person. It's roughly half, sometimes a third, of the price of cod and haddock, and most major supermarkets sell it in the frozen section. If your fillets are smaller, you can secure two together with cocktail sticks. Cornflour I prefer sometimes to normal flour when using a frozen defrosted product. I tend to find there is more water migration (thawed water) and cornflour sticks the batter to the fillet more evenly. The nutrition below includes the chips, mushy peas and tartare sauce (overleaf).

SERVES	PREP TIME	SOAK TIME	COOK TIME
4	30 MINS	12 HRS	40–50 MINS

ENERGY (KCALS)	PROTEIN	FAT	SATURATED FAT	CARB.	TOTAL SUGARS	SALT	FIBRE
682	39	14	1.5	93	5	1.9	16

Fish

vegetable oil, for deep frying

250g self-raising flour

pinch of freshly ground black pepper

400ml sparkling water

4 × 100g skinned, boneless frozen pollock fillets (or whiting, haddock or gurnard), defrosted

3–4 tablespoons cornflour, for dusting

Fill a large saucepan with oil and heat until the oil reaches 185°C on a cooking thermometer.

Place the flour and pepper into a bowl, then add enough sparkling water to form a smooth batter, not too thick. Dust two fillets in cornflour, then carefully place into the batter one at a time. Coat well and place straight into the hot oil. Cook no more than two at a time or the oil temperature will drop too much. Deep-fry for 7–8 minutes, stirring occasionally until golden.

Lift out of the oil and drain well, let the oil come back to temperature and cook the remaining fillets. Serve with chips, mushy peas and tartare sauce (see below and overleaf).

Chips

700g potatoes (King Edwards or Maris Pipers work well), peeled and cut into chunky chips, then washed

2 tablespoons any oil

salt (ideally sea salt)

Preheat the oven to 220°C/gas 7.

Place the chips into a pan and cover with cold water. Add a little salt (this helps to brown in the oven) and bring to the boil, then simmer for 5–6 minutes, or until half cooked (do not overcook or they will fall apart).

Drain in a colander, then carefully place onto a non-stick baking tray. Pour over the oil and coat the chips well. Place into the oven and cook for 20–30 minutes to crisp up and take on a little colour.

MUSHY PEAS

225g dried green or
marrowfat peas, soaked
overnight in cold water
salt and freshly ground
black pepper

Rinse the soaked peas well, then place into a saucepan. Just cover with cold water, and then bring to the boil. Skim well, then simmer for 20–25 minutes until the peas are soft and just falling apart and the liquid has mostly evaporated.

Mix well with a wooden spoon or potato masher, and season with a little salt and pepper. The end result should be, nice and soft thick texture but not smooth. Cover and keep warm.

TARTARE SAUCE

1 tablespoon capers, drained
and roughly chopped
2 gherkins, roughly chopped
½ each turnip and onion, peeled
and finely chopped
4 tablespoons 0% fat thick yogurt
4 tablespoons chopped
fresh parsley
squeeze of lemon juice

Mix together the capers, gherkins, turnip and onion then add the parsley and lemon juice, and mix well. Season with pepper and add just enough yogurt to bind everything together well.

TIP

Peas may be higher in carbs and sugar than other vegetables, but they contain phytonutrients that can help reduce inflammation and have antioxidant properties. Unlike in some recipes for mushy peas, I don't add bicarbonate of soda as it can damage the minerals and vitamins.

Pot-roasting is part roasting and part braising, so it's roasting in a covered environment, if that makes sense. Not only do you get a fabulously tender chicken but also you get the best gravy! The nutrition below includes the roast potatoes and one Yorkshire pudding per person; just freeze the extra ones for your next roast.

PROPER POT-ROAST CHICKEN

£7.13

ENERGY (KCALS)	PROTEIN	FAT	SATURATED FAT	CARB.	TOTAL SUGARS	SALT	FIBRE
775	57.5	30.5	4	61	18.5	1.5	3.4

SERVES	PREP TIME	COOK TIME
4	15	60-75
	MINS	MINS + 30 MINS RESTING

Preheat the oven to 220°C/gas 7.

Place the chicken into a deep, ovenproof saucepan or baking dish. Pop into the oven and leave for about 15 minutes, or until it takes on a little colour.

Remove from the oven and place the vegetables around the bird, along with the stock cube and about 300ml of water. Reduce the oven temperature to 200°C/gas 6. Return to the oven cook for 45 minutes to 1 hour – do not overcook.

Once cooked, carefully lift out the chicken with two forks and place on a large plate, then cover with cling film and leave to rest for 30 minutes.

To make the gravy, strain the stock from the vegetables into a bowl, and leave to settle so the fat separates. Carefully skim off the fat, then place the stock into a small saucepan over a medium heat and bring to a simmer. Mix the cornflour with 4 tablespoons of water, then stir into the simmering mixture. Stir constantly until the juices thicken nicely, but don't go mad. Season to taste.

Meanwhile, cover the cabbage on a microwave-safe plate and cook in the microwave on full power for four bursts of 3 minutes.

Joint the chicken on a large plate and serve with the braised vegetables and cabbage, roast potatoes and Yorkshire pudding (overleaf).

1.3kg fresh whole chicken

2 onions, each chopped into 6

1 swede, cut into small chunks

2 carrots, cut into small chunks

1 leek, cut into small chunks

2 celery sticks, cut into small chunks

½ × 10g reduced-salt chicken stock cube, crumbled

1 sweetheart cabbage, quartered

For the gravy

2 tablespoons cornflour

salt (optional)

freshly ground black pepper

ROAST POTATOES

Preheat the oven to 200°C/gas 6.

Pour the oil into a baking tray and place in the oven to get very hot, about 10 minutes.

Place the potatoes into a saucepan filled with water and bring to the boil, then simmer for about 20 minutes until the potato starts to soften and crumble at the edges: this is very important, as the finished potatoes will be much crispier if they start to fall apart at this stage. Strain in a colander and leave to steam for 2 minutes, shaking occasionally.

Carefully remove the hot tray from the oven, then add the potatoes and season well with salt and pepper. Roast in the oven for 25 minutes, then turn over and roast for a further 30 minutes. If you want crunchy edges, you may have to leave them slightly longer, but do not turn them again. That's it: simple and fail-safe, perfect roast tatties.

100ml vegetable oil
600g peeled potatoes,
   such as Maris Piper, King Edward,
   Cara, cut into chunks about the
   size of a large plum
salt and freshly ground
   black pepper

MY YORKSHIRE PUDDING

Preheat the oven to 200°C/gas 6.

In a bowl, place the flour, eggs and half the milk and mix to a smooth batter, then gradually mix in the remaining milk. Add 2 tablespoons of oil to each hole of a 12-hole muffin tin and pop into the oven on a baking tray to heat up. After 10 minutes, remove from the oven.

Season the Yorkshire pudding batter, then pour into the hot tin, filling each hole no more than three-quarters. Immediately return to the oven. Cook for 10 minutes, then reduce the heat to 180°C/gas 4. Cook for around a further 40 minutes, or until well risen and golden brown. When they look ready, allow 10 more minutes in the oven before removing.

MAKES

 12

113g plain flour
2 medium eggs, at room
   temperature
300ml skimmed milk
vegetable oil
salt

Any form of curry can be rather calorific as it's generally cooked in ghee (clarified butter), but this version gives you the great curry flavour kick and satisfaction with fewer calories and less salt. Using skinned and boned chicken breast cuts down the fat, though it can go dry if overcooked; to avoid this I use the Chinese 'velveting' technique of marinating in cornflour and egg white, then blanching to keep the breast juicy and moist. The nutrition below includes the carrot raita (overleaf).

ENERGY (KCALS)	PROTEIN	FAT	SATURATED FAT	CARB.	TOTAL SUGARS	SALT	FIBRE
270	31	7	4.5	18.5	10.5	1.4	4.5

SERVES	PREP TIME	COOK TIME
4	15 MINS	12-15 MINS

In a bowl, whisk together the egg white, starch and black pepper, and then add the chicken. Mix well and set aside while you make the curry sauce.

Place the onion, garlic, cardamom pods, mango chutney, coconut, ginger, chilli, tomatoes, tomato purée, turmeric, cumin and stock cube into a food-processor and blitz to a nice paste.

Bring a shallow pan of salted water to the boil. Once boiling, drop in the chicken pieces and stir to stop the starch from sticking, then bring back to a simmer. Immediately lift out with a slotted spoon and place into a clean saucepan.

Pour over the curry paste and bring to the boil, then reduce the heat and simmer for 12–14 minutes; the curry may well cook in less time.

Once cooked, check the seasoning and adjust if needed. Remove from the heat and stir in the lemon juice, coriander and yogurt. Serve with rice and raita (see overleaf).

1 medium egg white, lightly beaten

2 heaped tablespoons starch (cornflour, arrowroot, etc.)

pinch of black pepper

3 medium chicken breasts, skinned and cut into 1cm strips

For the sauce

1 large onion, very finely chopped

2 garlic cloves, peeled

4 cardamom pods, crushed

1 tablespoon mango chutney

2 tablespoons desiccated coconut

2 heaped tablespoons finely chopped fresh ginger

1 heaped teaspoon chopped red chilli

8 ripe (good flavoured) fresh tomatoes

1 tablespoon tomato purée

½ teaspoon turmeric

½ teaspoon ground cumin

10g chicken stock cube

juice of ½ lemon

20g freshly chopped coriander

3 tablespoons thick natural yogurt

CARROT RAITA

SERVES

 4

PREP
TIME

 10

MINS

½ teaspoon ground cumin, toasted

pinch of chilli flakes

½ teaspoon ground turmeric

250ml low-fat natural yogurt

2 tablespoons tamarind purée or
   the juice of 2 limes

2 large organic carrots,
   roughly grated

2 tablespoons fresh mint,
   finely chopped

salt and freshly ground black
   pepper

Mix everything together apart from the carrots and mint. Taste to see if you are happy, and adjust any of the ingredients if necessary. Pour over the carrots, mix well and add the mint, then cover. If you can leave at room temperature for 1 hour, all the better.

Remix and taste, then season again if needed, and serve with the curry (see page 119).

TIP

Chicken is a great low-fat option meat, but also lean pork, turkey, venison and game such as pheasant would work well in this recipe.

I like this dish; it looks very impressive and shows how you can cook vegetables to get the best flavour from them. Some chefs add pancakes to their Wellington, but I think it can make the dish heavy and sodden. I bake my beetroot in foil in a moderate oven for 45 minutes or thereabouts rather than boil them, as I think the beetroot flavour is far more intense that way. If you are making the coriander sauce, then cook the extra beetroots before you start. The nutrition below includes the beetroot coriander sauce (overleaf).

ENERGY (KCALS)	PROTEIN	FAT	SATURATED FAT	CARB.	TOTAL SUGARS	SALT	FIBRE
727	16	40.5	17	71	15	1.8	8

SERVES	PREP TIME	COOK TIME
4	45 MINS	1.5 HRS

Place the mushrooms and onions into a food-processor and blitz, not too finely.

Heat the oil in a wok or large frying pan over a low heat, add the garlic, mushrooms and tomato purée and season. Cook for 15–20 minutes, or until very dry: you need to get all the moisture out.

When very dry, remove the wok from the heat and cool slightly. Add enough breadcrumbs to make a stiff paste, and then chill well.

Roll out half the puff pastry to roughly 30 × 12cm, and then place on a greased baking tray (this saves you lifting later). Spoon on half the mushroom mixture and flatten slightly, leaving 2–3cm on each side.

Cut roughly a quarter off one side of each beetroot. Place the four beetroot on the mushroom purée, with a slight space in between. Cover the beetroot in a thin layer of the mushroom purée.

Roll out the other half of the pastry to 25 × 35cm, large enough to cover the beetroot and mushroom mix. Brush the outside edge of the base pastry with beaten egg, then carefully lay the second piece of pastry on top, pressing down and sealing the edges well. Lightly press around the beetroot and in between, so you can see the beetroot shape and the finished wellington looks tight.

Decorate and tidy up the bottom edge, then brush with beaten egg, and chill in the fridge for 1 hour.

Continued overleaf...

250g chestnut mushrooms

2 small onions, finely chopped

2 tablespoons any oil

2 garlic cloves, crushed

1 heaped tablespoon tomato purée

6–8 heaped tablespoons dried breadcrumbs

500g puff pastry

4 large beetroot, peeled and cooked (see recipe introduction)

1 egg, beaten

salt and freshly ground black pepper

BEETROOT WELLINGTON CONTINUED

Preheat the oven to 200°C/gas 6.

Bake in the oven for 35–40 minutes, or until well browned and cooked through.

Remove and leave for a further 10–15 minutes to rest.

Cut into four between each beetroot and serve with the beetroot coriander sauce (see below).

BEETROOT CORIANDER SAUCE

1 teaspoon any oil

1 red onion, finely chopped

2 garlic cloves, chopped

2 teaspoons tomato purée

½ × 10g vegetable stock cube

400g cooked beetroot (see recipe introduction on page 121), cut into 5mm cubes

4 tablespoons 0% fat thick yogurt or quark

4 tablespoons chopped fresh coriander

freshly ground black pepper

Heat the oil in a non-stick frying pan over a medium heat. Add the onion and garlic, then cook over a low heat for 2–3 minutes, or until they take on a little colour on the edges.

Stir in the tomato purée, 200ml of water and the stock cube and bring to the boil. Add the beetroot and simmer gently for 10 minutes until the stock is well reduced and coating the beetroot nicely but not too thickly.

Check the seasoning and adjust if needed: you will only need pepper. Remove from the heat once thickened and leave to cool for 2–3 minutes. Stir in the yogurt or quark and coriander and serve with the sliced Wellington (see above).

CHEAT'S PAELLA

£8.59

This is not a truly authentic paella but it's a pretty good version using frozen seafood. It's quick and easy to make, and looks pretty good. You can serve this as a main course or, if you prefer, divide it into eight and serve as a starter.

SERVES	PREP TIME	COOK TIME
4	20 MINS	20 MINS

ENERGY (KCALS)	PROTEIN	FAT	SATURATED FAT	CARB.	TOTAL SUGARS	SALT	FIBRE
628	30.5	15.5	2.5	90	10	2.4	5

4 tablespoons extra virgin olive oil

2 small onions, finely chopped

4 garlic cloves, finely chopped

1 red pepper, cut into 1cm pieces

1 yellow pepper, cut into 1cm
   pieces

2 tablespoons tomato purée

350g paella rice

2 chicken thighs, skinned, boned
   and cut into thin strips

500g bag frozen seafood (squid,
   mussels, prawns, etc.)

1 teaspoon smoked paprika

½ teaspoon ground turmeric

600ml boiling water

½ × 10g reduced-salt vegetable
   stock cube, crumbled

2 heaped tablespoons roughly
   chopped fresh parsley

salt and freshly ground black
   pepper

Preheat the oven to 200°C/gas 6.

Heat the oil in an ovenproof frying pan over a medium heat, and then add the onions, garlic and peppers. Fry for 10 minutes so the peppers release their colour slightly, then add the tomato purée. Add the rice and coat well in the oil and onion mixture. Add the chicken pieces and the seafood, along with the paprika and turmeric, mixing really well.

Add the boiling water and stock cube, then season with a little salt and pepper and mix really well. Bring back to the boil, cover with a tight-fitting lid, then pop into the oven. Cook for 15 minutes.

Remove from the oven, remove the lid and stir well. Add the parsley. You may want to add a little more olive oil here, too. Cover and leave for 10 minutes, then serve.

TIP

Seafood is low in saturated fat, and choosing frozen can be not only cheaper but also more nutritious than fresh, as it is frozen as soon as it is caught, which preserves the minerals and vitamins.

I'm not sure whether this dish originated in India or Glasgow, but this ever-popular offering can be seen on pretty much every takeaway menu in the land. I have reduced the fat and salt content, adding spices and herbs to compensate. From a price point of view, I have added a chapatti recipe, if you fancy having a go at making your own.

NATION'S FAVOURITE DISH

CHICKEN TIKKA MASALA

£6.01

ENERGY (KCALS)	PROTEIN	FAT	SATURATED FAT	CARB.	TOTAL SUGARS	SALT	FIBRE
537	38.5	11.5	1.5	66	10.5	0.6	8

SERVES	PREP TIME	COOK TIME
4	15 MINS	20-25 MINS

Wash the rice in a colander until the water runs clear. Soak in a bowl of warm water (boiled and cooled) for 30 minutes.

Meanwhile, velvet the chicken by mixing together the cornflour and egg white, then add the chicken and mix well.

Place all the paste ingredients except the oil into a small food-processor and blitz to a paste. Heat the oil in a non-stick wok over a medium heat, then add the paste and cook for 10 minutes until it takes on a nice colour. Add the chicken, increase the heat to high and cook for 2–3 minutes to quickly seal the meat.

Blitz the tomatoes and sugar, if using, with a stick blender or in a blender. Pour over the chicken, then gently simmer for 15 minutes, stirring occasionally, to thicken.

Meanwhile, place the soaked rice into a saucepan and just cover with cold water, then add the turmeric and cardamom pods. Bring to the boil and then simmer according to the packet instructions.

To make the chapattis, sift together the flour and salt in a bowl. Stir in the olive oil and 60ml of water, and then knead until firm and elastic. Divide into four balls and roll out as flat as possible. Heat a frying or griddle pan over a medium–high heat. Cook the chapatti for about 1–2 minutes per side until blistered and puffed.

Remove the curry from the heat and leave to cool for 5 minutes, then stir in the yogurt. Serve in deep bowls with a few coriander leaves sprinkled over.

2 tablespoons cornflour

1 medium egg white

400g skinless chicken breast, fat-removed, chopped

400g can tomatoes

pinch of sugar (optional)

150g 0% fat natural yogurt

4 tablespoons fresh coriander leaves, to serve

For the rice

400g basmati rice

¼ teaspoon ground turmeric

6 cardamom pods, crushed

For the paste

1 tablespoon very finely chopped fresh ginger

5 garlic cloves, peeled

1 small red chilli, chopped

3 tablespoons tikka curry powder

2 onions, very finely chopped

2 tablespoons any oil

For the chapatti

125g wholemeal flour

pinch of salt

1 tablespoon olive oil

If you wish to make your own curry paste, mix together 1 teaspoon chilli, 2 teaspoons cumin, 1 teaspoon garam masala, 4 bay leaves, 10 cardamom pods, 1 teaspoon cinnamon, ½ teaspoon mace and 10 cloves. Lightly toast in a dry frying pan, then finely grind.

I love this recipe: it's a mix of four or five recipes I have picked up over the years and from many a long discussion with my great friend and chef-restauranteur Reza Mahammad. This one-pot dish has such a deep flavour and texture that it's become a real go-to dish when I need comfort food with a bit of a kick! Some recipes add rose water and more dried fruits, and a lot are made with goat and lamb. Here I use chicken purely for convenience, plus it will cook in only 20–25 minutes.

CHICKEN BIRYANI

£9.71

ENERGY (KCALS)	PROTEIN	FAT	SATURATED FAT	CARB.	TOTAL SUGARS	SALT	FIBRE
747	49	19	3	92	20	2.2	5.5

SERVES	PREP TIME	COOK TIME
4	30 MINS	20-25 MINS

Mix the paste together with the yogurt, then add the chicken. In an ovenproof pan (not too large but deep enough for the meat and vegetables to be layered tightly) heat the oil over a medium heat. Add the cumin seeds and ginger and cook quickly, then add the onions and cook for 4–5 minutes to get some good colour.

Add the chicken thighs and cook on both sides for 2–3 minutes, or until they get a little colour. Add the tomatoes and cook for a further 2 minutes. Add half the soaked rice, stir well, then sprinkle over the coriander, mint and raisins. Add the rest of the rice and pack down nicely. Pour over the hot stock, bring to the boil, then turn down to the tiniest simmer. Cover with a tight-fitting lid and cook for 15 minutes (resist the temptation to open).

After 15 minutes, check to see if the rice is cooked and the liquid soaked up, then dot with more coriander. When cooked, cover and leave for 20 minutes to rest.

Serve topped with flaked almonds, crispy fried onions and ginger strips, if using, and large sprigs of coriander.

5 tablespoons biryani paste (or see opposite to make your own)

100g thick natural yogurt

8 medium chicken thighs, bone in, skinned

4 tablespoons any oil

1 tablespoon cumin seeds

2 tablespoons finely chopped ginger

2 small onions, finely chopped

2 large tomatoes, chopped

350g basmati rice, washed well and soaked for 30 minutes

4 tablespoons chopped fresh coriander

2 tablespoons chopped fresh mint

75g raisins, soaked in boiling water

800ml hot chicken stock

To serve
coriander leaves
toasted flaked almonds (optional)
crispy fried onions (optional)
crispy fried ginger strips (optional)

GREEN MASSAMAN CURRY

£5.46

SERVES	PREP TIME	COOK TIME
4	25	25
	MINS	MINS

This fragrant curry is a delicious alternative to a chicken, beef or fish version. The light stock is really packed full of flavour, plus using plenty of vegetables really makes this quite a substantial meal once you add rice. I tend to use frozen vegetables quite a lot in curries, braises or stews purely because they break down nicely to help thicken the end sauce. It's also convenient to have them there all the time.

ENERGY (KCALS)	PROTEIN	FAT	SATURATED FAT	CARB.	TOTAL SUGARS	SALT	FIBRE
496	11	19	7.5	65.5	16	1.1	9

2 tablespoons any oil

2 medium onions, finely chopped

4 garlic cloves, finely chopped

1–2 tablespoons Green massaman
   curry paste

400g can reduced-fat coconut milk

10g vegetable stock cube

500g potatoes, chopped into
   chunks the size of a walnut (use a
   serrated potato chopper)

1 teaspoon palm or light brown
   sugar

juice of 2 Kaffir limes (or normal
   ones), plus extra wedges to serve

4–5 tablespoons tamarind juice

dash of light soy sauce

100ml pineapple juice (optional)

200g baby spinach leaves

200g frozen peas

200g green beans, cut into 2cm
   pieces (blanched and refreshed
   or frozen are fine)

2 tablespoons roasted peanuts,
   toasted and chopped

2 tablespoons Thai basil, shredded

salt (optional)

Heat the oil in a frying pan over a medium heat. Add the onions and garlic and cook for 4–5 minutes until you get a nice golden colour.

Add the curry paste and warm through, then add the coconut milk, stock cube and about 150ml of water. Bring to the boil, and then add the potatoes, palm sugar, lime juice, tamarind juice, soy and pineapple juice, if using. Simmer for 15 minutes until they are just cooked.

Season with a little salt but be careful as a lot of premade pastes are highly seasoned. Once the potatoes are cooked, add the spinach and wilt, then add the peas, beans and peanuts and warm through. Serve with shredded Thai basil, Jasmine or sticky rice and wedges of lime.

Green vegetables are packed with vitamins, minerals and fibre and leafy green vegetables, such as spinach, have particularly high levels of antioxidants, which protect your cells from the effects of free radicals, which can cause illness and premature ageing.

CAULIFLOWER WITH CURRIED LENTILS

£4.58

I will never go back to boiling cauliflower again, even for cauliflower cheese. The intense flavour you get when roasting is so much better and really makes the whole dish. Here, after roasting I spoon over curried lentils. I use canned lentils for convenience, but by all means cook fresh; even some of the new microwave packs are pretty good, but they're a little more expensive.

SERVES	PREP TIME	COOK TIME
4	20 MINS	40 MINS

ENERGY (KCALS)	PROTEIN	FAT	SATURATED FAT	CARB.	TOTAL SUGARS	SALT	FIBRE
483	19	26	4	36.5	15	2.6	14

For the cauliflower

2 medium cauliflowers, cut into
    small florets

4 tablespoons olive oil

2 teaspoons ground turmeric

salt and freshly ground black
    pepper

For the lentils

2 teaspoons cumin seeds

2 teaspoons fenugreek

8 cardamom pods, crushed

2 teaspoons garam masala

4 tablespoons any oil

2 medium onions, finely chopped

4 garlic cloves, finely chopped

2 × 400g cans cooked green lentils,
    drained

10g vegetable stock cube,
    crumbled

Preheat the oven to 220°C/gas 7.

Place the cauliflower into a bowl. In a separate bowl, mix together the oil and turmeric with some salt and pepper. Pour over the cauliflower and mix really well. Place the cauliflower into a baking dish or tray and roast in the oven for 25–35 minutes, stirring occasionally: you want a really nice colour to the florets.

Meanwhile, dry-fry the spices in a frying pan over a medium heat to release their flavour and toast slightly – do not burn.

Add the oil, onions and garlic and cook for 5 minutes, then add the lentils and just enough water to cover them. Add the stock cube, some ground pepper and a little salt, if needed. Mix well, bring to the boil and simmer for 10 minutes, or until the mix thickens and reduces. I sometimes break it up a little with a potato masher to make the sauce slightly thicker.

Once the cauliflower is cooked, spoon into four deep bowls, then spoon over the curried lentils.

TIP

You don't need to add any carbohydrates here, as the lentils will be plenty filling and a great source of protein and fibre.

I like tofu in all ways and dishes; it's a great vehicle for adding flavour. Here we have a sweet and sour taste profile with tomatoes and tamarind, which is balanced by semi-dry dates. The smokiness of the tofu adds another layer of flavour.

SMOKED TOFU & SPICED LENTILS

£4.58

ENERGY (KCALS)	PROTEIN	FAT	SATURATED FAT	CARB.	TOTAL SUGARS	SALT	FIBRE
659	25.5	21	3.5	88	11	1.3	7

SERVES	PREP TIME	COOK TIME
4	15	45
	MINS	MINS

Boil the lentils in plenty of salted water for 10–12 minutes until soft, then drain well.

Heat 1 tablespoon of the oil in a pan over a medium heat. Cook the onion and carrot for 5 minutes to soften and then stir in the ginger, garlic, chilli, turmeric, tamarind paste and some pepper. Continue to cook for a couple of minutes and then add the tomatoes and dates. Partially cover the pan and cook gently for 15 minutes, adding 100ml of water if it looks dry.

Meanwhile, cut the smoked tofu into 1cm pieces and dry well on kitchen towel. Heat the remaining tablespoon of oil in a non-stick frying pan over a high heat, then add the tofu and sauté quickly until it takes on a little colour. Add the lentil mix to the tofu and warm through.

200g green lentils, soaked in cold
    water for 1 hour
2 tablespoons vegetable oil
1 medium onion, finely chopped
1 medium carrot, diced
2cm piece of fresh ginger, peeled
    and grated
2 garlic cloves, crushed to a paste
1 teaspoon chilli flakes
½ teaspoon ground turmeric
2 teaspoons tamarind paste
400g can chopped tomatoes
6–8 semi-dry dates, pitted
    and roughly chopped
400g smoked tofu
freshly ground black pepper

TIP

Spices are often overlooked in terms of their health benefits, but only a small amount can reap large benefits, such as reducing inflammation (turmeric, ginger and tamarind) and blood pressure (garlic), providing antioxidants and helping reduce appetite (chilli).

PUMPKIN & BLACK-EYED PEA PILAF

£6.95

For the best results with this recipe, roast the seasoned, oiled pumpkin really well in wedges. Don't be shy, and slightly overcook so they have some good colour and flavour. I love one-pot cooking and nothing typifies this more than a pilaf. Plus, once the rice and liquid are added it cooks in only 15–18 minutes.

SERVES	PREP TIME	COOK TIME
4	10 MINS	20 MINS

ENERGY (KCALS)	PROTEIN	FAT	SATURATED FAT	CARB.	TOTAL SUGARS	SALT	FIBRE
682	24	31	6	73	10	1.8	10.5

2 tablespoons olive oil

2 red onions, very finely sliced

1 teaspoon turmeric

2 teaspoons cumin seeds

500g roughly chopped well-roasted pumpkin flesh (see recipe introduction)

400g can black-eyed peas, drained

150g frozen peas

225g long grain rice

568ml (1 pint) boiling water

10g vegetable stock cube, crumbled

salt (optional)

freshly ground black pepper

For the paste

4 tablespoons roasted pumpkin seeds

6 tablespoons chopped fresh basil

50g Parmesan, roughly grated

4 tablespoons roughly chopped roasted pumpkin flesh (see recipe introduction)

4 tablespoons sun-dried tomatoes

4 tablespoons extra virgin olive oil

Heat the oil in a medium saucepan over a medium heat. Add the onion, turmeric and cumin seeds and cook for 3–4 minutes to soften.

Add the pumpkin flesh, black-eyed peas and frozen peas and mix well. Add the rice, boiling water and stock cube. Season well with salt, if using, and pepper, and then bring to the boil, stirring. Cover the pan with a tight-fitting lid, turn the heat right down, and cook really gently for roughly 12–15 minutes, or until the rice is cooked and the water absorbed. You will be amazed at how little heat is required, if you have a tight-fitting lid.

Meanwhile, blitz together all the ingredients for the paste, adding olive oil until you have a thick paste, season well.

Once the pilaf is cooked, remove the lid and fluff up with a spoon or fork, the fold through the paste and serve.

Pumpkin is packed with vitamin A, which is great for your eyesight and skin. And you won't miss meat here, as black-eyed peas are a very good source of protein and fibre.

TRAY-BAKED SALMON & TOMATOES

£14.60

SERVES	PREP TIME	COOK TIME	REST TIME
4	30 MINS	30 MINS	15 MINS

ENERGY (KCALS)	PROTEIN	FAT	SATURATED FAT	CARB.	TOTAL SUGARS	SALT	FIBRE
513	35	31.5	6.5	20	14.5	0.5	5

The secret to this dish is to half-cook the salmon and leave covered to finish off the cooking. It's very important you do not overcook the salmon, or the fish will be dry. I have used whole fresh fillet here, but frozen wild salmon portions work equally as well: they will only need 5–6 minutes to cook though.

2 tablespoons olive oil

385g can sweetcorn, drained

2 red onions, finely chopped

2 teaspoons fresh red chilli, finely chopped

200g baby spinach leaves

20 baby plum tomatoes, halved

600g middle fillet of salmon, skin-on but scaled (no pin bones)

juice of 3 limes

3–4 tablespoons chopped fresh coriander

3–4 tablespoons chopped fresh mint

3–4 tablespoons reduced-fat crème fraîche

1 tablespoon runny honey (optional)

salt and freshly ground black pepper

Preheat the oven to 230°C/gas 8.

Place the olive oil into a wok or deep frying or sauté pan over a high heat. Add the sweetcorn, red onion and chilli, then sauté quickly for 4–5 minutes until they take on a little colour. (This can be done way in advance.)

Spoon the sweetcorn mixture into a baking tray, then sprinkle over the spinach and place in the oven to cook for roughly 10–12 minutes.

Remove from the oven and add the tomatoes. Season the salmon fillet, then place on top. Squeeze over the lime juice and bake in the oven for a further 10 minutes – do not overcook.

With the salmon still half-cooked, remove the tray from the oven, cover with foil and leave to rest for 15 minutes. Carefully lift the salmon out of the tray using two fish slices and flake with a spoon.

Mix together the coriander, mint, crème fraîche and runny honey, if using, and season with salt and pepper. Stir into the cooked veg. Spoon the salmon into small deep bowls and top with the vegetable mix.

I got quite a bit of flack when I did this recipe on the telly, but I'm not really sure why. I was told it wasn't real cooking and that it was 'not cheffy enough', but I absolutely disagree. It just goes to prove that simple, everyday ingredients can work extremely well if put together carefully.

SIMPLE SPICY FUSILLI & SWEETCORN

£1.14

ENERGY (KCALS)	PROTEIN	FAT	SATURATED FAT	CARB.	TOTAL SUGARS	SALT	FIBRE
535	16	4	0.5	104	13	1.6	10

SERVES	PREP TIME	COOK TIME
2	15 MINS	15 MINS

Place the onion, garlic, chilli flakes and sweetcorn into a small saucepan and add the stock cube. Pour in the boiling water until level with the corn, then bring to the boil. Simmer for 5 minutes.

Mix the cornflour with 3 tablespoons of water, then stir this into the simmering corn until thickened. Pour into a blender and blitz until smooth. Pour this sauce over the warm pasta, season and stir well. Serve with a little sweet chilli sauce, if using.

1 small onion, chopped

2 garlic cloves, crushed

pinch of dried chilli flakes

365g can sweetcorn

½ × 10g vegetable stock cube

100ml boiling water

2 tablespoons cornflour

400g cooked fusilli

salt (optional)

freshly ground black pepper

sweet chilli sauce, to serve (optional)

TIP

A super healthy whole grain, corn is a good source of fibre, vitamin C and antioxidants that promote healthy vision.

ROASTED CHICKPEA & PEPPER POTS

£7.53

We have nice picnic, easy-eating food here. I tend to pack (and serve) this in small Kilner jars, which is something I normally shy away from. I'm not really into pretentious forms of food or presentation but in this instance, it works. Firstly, you have the great texture of the chickpeas, especially because you roast them. You can, of course, cook your own: it's up to you. Secondly, the use of quinoa, brown rice or even wild rice makes this dish a very healthy, fulfilling option.

SERVES	PREP TIME	COOK TIME
4	20 MINS	30 MINS

ENERGY (KCALS)	PROTEIN	FAT	SATURATED FAT	CARB.	TOTAL SUGARS	SALT	FIBRE
826	28	42	11	74	21	2.6	19

2 × 400g cans chickpeas, drained and dried

6 tablespoons olive oil

1 red onion, finely chopped

4 garlic cloves, finely chopped

3 red peppers, deseeded and cut into 2cm pieces

2 tablespoons tomato purée

2–3 tablespoons balsamic vinegar

250g sun-dried tomatoes, roughly chopped

200g buffalo mozzarella, ripped into small pieces

250g packet microwaveable quinoa, warmed

250g cooked brown basmati rice, warmed

salt and freshly ground black pepper

Preheat the oven to 200°C/gas 6.

Toss the chickpeas in half the oil, add a little salt and pepper and roast in the oven for 15 minutes until dry and with a little colour.

Meanwhile, heat the rest of the oil in a frying pan over a low heat and add the red onion, garlic and pepper pieces. Sauté slowly for 3–4 minutes until soft and with a little colour. Mix the tomato purée and vinegar together well, add to the peppers and cook for 1 minute.

Layer up small Kilner jars with the pepper mix, sun-dried tomatoes, mozzarella, cooked quinoa, rice and then chickpeas, seasoning as you go. Chill well before serving.

SOMETHING
SWEET

The addition of bananas gives these flapjacks a lovely soft texture and delicious flavour. Using the natural sweetness of the fruit means that you can use less sugar. The banana also helps to make the end flapjack nice and moist, meaning you can use less butter.

BANANA & PINE NUT FLAPJACKS

£2.81

ENERGY (KCALS)	PROTEIN	FAT	SATURATED FAT	CARB.	TOTAL SUGARS	SALT	FIBRE
244	4	10.5	5	32	12	TRACE	2.5

SERVES	PREP TIME	COOK TIME
12	20 MINS	30 MINS

Preheat the oven to 190°C/gas 5. Line a shallow, 23cm-square baking tin with greaseproof paper.

Place the butter, honey and sugar into a large pan and melt together over a medium heat. Or you can gently warm in a microwave for 3–4 minutes on medium setting.

Stir the oats, pine nuts and cinnamon into the melted mixture. Roughly mash the bananas with a fork, then add to the oat mix. Spoon into the lined tin, level and press down slightly. Bake in the oven for 20–25 minutes until golden; I tend to slightly undercook, otherwise the flapjack can become crunchy.

Remove and gently cut into 12 pieces three quarters of the way through, then leave to cool completely. Once cooled, finish cutting with a sharp knife.

100g salted butter

3 tablespoons runny honey

60g light brown sugar

350g porridge oats

50g pine nuts, lightly toasted

½ teaspoon ground cinnamon

2 large ripe bananas (approx. 250g)

TIP

Bananas may get a bad rap for being high in carbs and sugar, but they're much healthier alternatives to flour and are great sources of vitamin B6, manganese, potassium and fibre.

BANANAS & APRICOT SAUCE

£6.67

A simple, easy dessert that takes just a few minutes to prepare and cook.

SERVES	PREP TIME	COOK TIME
4	15 MINS	15 MINS

ENERGY (KCALS)	PROTEIN	FAT	SATURATED FAT	CARB.	TOTAL SUGARS	SALT	FIBRE
151	7	0	0	30	27	TRACE	2

220g can apricots in syrup, drained

4 large ripe bananas, peeled

1 vanilla pod, halved and deseeded

12 fresh Thai or conventional basil leaves

3–4 drops lemon oil or zest of 2 large lemons

200g low- or 0% fat yogurt

Preheat the oven to 230°C/gas 8.

Place the apricots into a blender, add a little water and blend into a thickish sauce.

Lay out four large pieces of foil. Place each banana onto a piece of foil, then fold up either end. On each banana, spoon over a quarter of the apricot sauce, a few vanilla seeds, three basil leaves and a drop of lemon oil.

Fold them up and seal well, place into a baking tray, then pour in 2cm of boiling water. Carefully place in the oven and cook for 10 minutes, depending on the ripeness of the bananas.

Serve warm with the foil parcels opened and a large blob of yogurt.

TIP

Bananas and apricots are so naturally sweet that you don't need to add any sugar here.

This is one of my favourite puddings of all time, in any guise. The secret is to make sure the crumble is two thirds of the finished dish, the other third being your chosen filling. The other thing to remember is to add the sugar to the crumble mix only after you have rubbed or blitzed in the butter to the flour. This stops the crumble becoming heavy and leaden like pastry.

APPLE & BLACKBERRY CRUMBLE

£5.44

ENERGY (KCALS)	PROTEIN	FAT	SATURATED FAT	CARB.	TOTAL SUGARS	SALT	FIBRE
792	8	29	18	107	56	0.6	7

SERVES	PREP TIME	COOK TIME
6	15	30
	MINS	MINS

Preheat the oven to 190°C/gas 5.

Place the apples, sugar and lemon zest and juice into a saucepan. Bring to the boil and then simmer for 5–6 minutes, or until the apples are half cooked, and remove from the heat.

Spoon carefully into a roughly 25cm-square, 5cm-deep baking dish. Sprinkle over the blackberries.

Place the cold butter and flour into a food-processor. Pulse until the mixture resembles fine breadcrumbs, then tip into a bowl. Using a spoon, mix in the sugar. (Working this way around ensures that the mixture does not cake up but keeps the crumble nice and loose.)

Spread lightly and evenly over the apples and blackberries, taking care not to pack down, so it is nice and domed. Bake in the oven for 25–30 minutes, or until golden.

Remove and cool before eating. I serve mine with warm custard.

4 large Bramley apples,
    peeled, cored and cut
    into medium chunks
150g caster sugar
zest and juice of 1 large lemon
250g fresh or frozen blackberries
200g cold salted butter
400g plain flour
100g caster sugar

TIP

Apples are excellent sources of antioxidants that help keep your brain healthy. Add in blackberries containing high levels of essential vitamin C and vitamin A (which helps support the immune system) and you've got a 'super' dessert.

CANNED CHERRY PIE

£3.55

SERVES	MAKES	PREP TIME	COOK TIME
6	1	30	40
	24CM X 4CM PIE	MINS	MINS

When I was little, we pretty much lived on canned fruit such as pears, peaches and fruit cocktail with evaporated milk. At school, we had a cherry pie made using canned cherries that was one of the few puddings that I liked. When I started my first cooking job in a pub, the chef cooked (I use that term carefully) duck with cherries: the dish consisted of half a roast Cherry Valley duck warmed in the oven with a can of cherries spooned over... Strange that, as it may sound as if I rather like good-quality canned cherries; in a pie they are quite good.

ENERGY (KCALS)	PROTEIN	FAT	SATURATED FAT	CARB.	TOTAL SUGARS	SALT	FIBRE
515	7	27.2	10	59	24	0.5	3.7

500g shortcrust or dessert pastry

2 × 400g cans good-quality black cherries, drained (reserve some juice)

2 tablespoons any brown sugar

2 tablespoons cornflour

1 medium egg, beaten

granulated sugar, for sprinkling

Preheat the oven to 180°C/gas 4. Cut the pastry into two circles – one 30cm, one 26cm (use your flan case as a guide, allowing extra pastry for the overhang). Line a 24cm loose-bottomed flan case with one of the discs of pastry, leaving a good overhang.

Place the cherries into a saucepan and add a little of the reserved juice, then add the sugar and mix well. Place the saucepan over a medium heat to warm.

In a bowl, mix the cornflower with 4 tablespoons of water and then add a little to thicken the cherries: they should be a very thick, creamy consistency. Once thick, cool for 15 minutes.

Pour the cherry mixture into the lined tart, and moisten the edges with a little beaten egg. Top with the second disc of pastry and seal the edges well. Cut off any excess pastry and crimp decoratively.

Brush with more beaten egg and sprinkle with sugar. Make three small incisions in the top of the pie and place in the oven. Bake for 30–40 minutes until the top of the pie is golden.

Remove from the oven and cool before eating. Cut into wedges and serve.

HARRY REDKNAPP'S ROLY POLY

£2.97

I cooked this specially for Mr Redknapp when he came onto ITV's *This Morning* programme having won *I'm a Celebrity Get Me Out of Here*. That was the food he missed the most while in the jungle, apparently. He did like the pudding very much! If you have any leftover roll, wrap it in cling film and chill in the fridge. When needed, slice while cold and warm gently in a microwave on medium power; take care though, as the jam could burn.

SERVES	PREP TIME	COOK TIME		ENERGY (KCALS)	PROTEIN	FAT	SATURATED FAT	CARB.	TOTAL SUGARS	SALT	FIBRE
4	20 MINS	40 MINS		686	12.5	24	13	104	46	0.8	2.5

225g self-raising flour

100g vegetarian suet

50g caster sugar

1 medium egg, lightly beaten

150g reduced-sugar blackcurrant jam

butter, for greasing

For the custard

568ml skimmed milk

4 heaped tablespoons custard powder

3–4 tablespoons sugar

Preheat the oven to 190°C/gas 5.

Place the flour, suet, sugar and egg into a bowl and mix well. Add a touch of cold water and mix to a soft but not sticky dough.

Roll out the pastry until it measures about 30 × 40cm. Spread over the jam thickly; there is nothing worse than an under-filled roll. Roll up lightly, not too tight, then cut in half, so you end up with two manageable rolls.

Tear off two pieces of foil, each roughly 30 × 40cm. Butter really well, then carefully place each pastry roll on top. Roll loosely around the pastry (it will expand when baking), then twist up the ends of each roll.

Scrunch up a large piece of foil and place in a baking tray, then place the rolls on top, making sure they do not touch the tray. Bake in the oven for 35–40 minutes, turning the rolls after 20 minutes. This ensures an even cook and colour at the end.

To test the roly polys are done, just gently squeeze and they should be full and firm. If not, then bake for a few more minutes. Once cooked, carefully remove from the oven and leave the rolls to set.

Meanwhile, make the custard by mixing roughly 100ml of the milk with the custard powder. Put the rest of the milk in a pan and bring to the boil, then quickly whisk in the custard milk mixture and bring back to a simmer to thicken. Remove from the heat and stir in the sugar to taste.

Open the foil roll and slice the roly poly. Serve with hot custard.

The suet and sugar content is ten per cent less than traditional roly poly, and reduced-sugar jam makes this overall a lower calorie version.

The texture of this finished cake really is a joy, however once you have cooked the cake you must leave it for at least 15–20 minutes, due to the fact that you are using half flour, half almonds. If you don't let it rest for this time, it will be quite difficult to cut. I have tried making this cake using ripe plums and even mango instead of the cherry. Here, I serve with plain yogurt, but reduced-fat crème fraîche also works well, or you can enjoy it on its own.

GLAZED ALMOND CHERRY CAKE

£11.92

ENERGY (KCALS)	PROTEIN	FAT	SATURATED FAT	CARB.	TOTAL SUGARS	SALT	FIBRE
592	12.3	34.5	16.1	57.3	42.5	0.9	1.6

SERVES	MAKES	PREP TIME	COOK TIME
8	23 CM CAKE	25 MINS	50-60 MINS

Heat oven to 160°C/gas 3.

Line a 23cm round, spring-form tin with greaseproof paper, making sure the paper comes about 3cm up the side of the tin. (This holds in the juice as the cake cooks.) Lightly grease the paper.

Spoon the jam over the bottom of the tin, then add the cherries in an even layer.

Beat the butter, sugar and vanilla together well for 2–3 minutes – no need to go mad. Beat in the eggs, then gently beat in the almonds and flour, and spoon nicely and evenly over the cherries.

Place the tin on a baking tray, just in case you get a leak, and bake for 50 minutes or until lightly browned. Once cooked, remove from the oven and leave to set for 15–20 minutes.

Carefully remove the outside ring and invert onto a large plate. Serve at room temperature with a little yogurt and vanilla extract mixed together.

220g salted butter or margarine, softened, plus extra for greasing
4 tablespoons reduced-sugar cherry jam
600g large cherries, pitted
220g caster sugar
2 teaspoons vanilla extract
4 medium eggs, at room temperature
120g ground almonds
150g self-raising flour

To serve
330ml reduced-fat plain yogurt
1 teaspoon vanilla extract

SOFT RASPBERRY CAKES

£3.09

This is a nice, easy cookie-cake recipe made using granulated sweetener. You can use conventional sugar if you prefer; just replace the sweetener with 75g caster sugar, though this will significantly increase the calories. Don't try and eat straight from the oven as they need time to rest, otherwise they will fall apart.

MAKES	PREP TIME	COOK TIME		ENERGY (KCALS)	PROTEIN	FAT	SATURATED FAT	CARB.	TOTAL SUGARS	SALT	FIBRE
8	15 MINS	20 MINS		232	5	10	3.5	30	1	0.5	3

85g margarine or butter

225g wholemeal flour

1 level teaspoon bicarb of soda

1 level teaspoon baking powder

1 medium egg, beaten

90g granulated sweetener

16 frozen raspberries

Preheat the oven to 200°C /gas 6.

Rub the margarine or butter into the flour then add the bicarb and baking powder. Add the egg and sweetener and mix together really well.

Form the mixture into eight balls roughly the size of large walnuts. Place onto a silicone baking tray leaving a good gap in between (they will spread slightly when baking) and press down slightly. Make two small indentations in the top, then push in the frozen raspberries. Reform the edges, raising them slightly around the raspberries and bake for 20 minutes.

Remove from the oven and cool completely, before attempting to lift off the sheet.

TIP

Frozen berries are just as nutritious as fresh but can cost half the price, especially in winter, and are available all year round.

Another simple tray bake, this also works well with raspberries, blueberries, loganberries and blackberries. A good tip, when washing strawberries, is to lightly rinse them in a colander, and then remove the stalk. This way the strawberries do not fill with water and will not go soggy. I tend to use oils a lot more in cakes, muffins and biscuits or cookies now instead of fats like butter or margarine. I feel in some instances you can get a lighter texture.

ALMOND & STRAWBERRY TRAY BAKE

£8.82

ENERGY (KCALS)	PROTEIN	FAT	SATURATED FAT	CARB.	TOTAL SUGARS	SALT	FIBRE
505	12.5	30	3.5	44	24	0.3	3.5

SERVES	PREP TIME	COOK TIME
8	10 MINS	25-30 MINS

Preheat the oven to 190°C/gas 5. Line a 24 × 18cm, 4cm deep baking tray with greaseproof paper.

Place the flour, brown sugar and ground almonds into a bowl and mix well. In a jug, beat the milk, egg and oil together well, then add this to the flour and sugar mixture and stir together. Do not overwork the mixture.

Spoon half the mixture into the baking tray. Dot over the strawberries, then spoon over the rest of the cake mix. Sprinkle over the flaked almonds. Bake for 25–30 minutes, or until well browned and risen.

Remove from the oven and leave to cool for 10 minutes. Turn out onto a tray, cut and serve with extra strawberries.

200g self-raising flour
150g light brown sugar
100g ground almonds
180ml skimmed milk
1 medium egg, beaten
125ml extra virgin olive oil
500g ripe, firm strawberries, halved
150g flaked almonds

Olive oil has countless health benefits; with lots of antioxidants, anti-inflammatory properties and monounsaturated fats, it can protect against heart disease, stroke and many other diseases and illnesses.

This cake is a bit of work, but well worth the effort. I have used an egg replacer that is starch based and works really well. You can find egg replacer at health food shops or online. This cake does have a firmer texture than a conventional cake, but adding date purée and topping with pine nuts adds a really nice flavour and texture.

APPLE, OIL & PINE NUT VEGAN CAKE

£3.43

ENERGY (KCALS)	PROTEIN	FAT	SATURATED FAT	CARB.	TOTAL SUGARS	SALT	FIBRE
226	4.6	8.2	1	31.7	16.5	0.5	3.3

MAKES	PREP TIME	COOK TIME
10 SLICES	20 MINS	45-50 MINS

Preheat the oven to 160°C/gas 3. Line a 2lb loaf tin with greaseproof loaf liner.

Place the apples into a small saucepan and add 50ml of cold water. Place over a medium heat and warm for 5–6 minutes until pulpy but not cooked, then cool slightly.

Put the date purée, sugar and oil into the bowl of an electric mixer and beat until smooth. Mix the egg replacer well with 90ml of cold water, then add this to the bowl and mix in. Next place the apple pulp into the date, oil and sugar mixture, then mix well.

In a separate bowl, mix together the flour and baking powder really well. Add the flour to the apple and oil mixture and beat together very quickly. Mix everything well, but don't overmix or the end sponge will be tough and chewy.

Spoon into the prepared loaf tin and spread out evenly, then sprinkle over the pine nuts. Place in the oven and cook for 45–50 minutes, or until well risen and cooked through.

Remove and cool on a wire rack for at least 20 minutes, then lift out and cool completely before trying to cut (with no egg you have a more fragile sponge).

1 large Bramley apple,
   peeled, cored and chopped
   (250g prepared)
75g date purée
95g caster sugar
50ml extra virgin olive oil
3 teaspoons (12g) egg replacer
220g wholemeal flour
4½ level teaspoons (14g)
   baking powder
50g pine nuts

SUGAR-FREE MERINGUES

£3.15

MAKES	PREP TIME	COOK TIME
10	10 MINS	25-30 MINS

ENERGY (KCALS)	PROTEIN	FAT	SATURATED FAT	CARB.	TOTAL SUGARS	SALT	FIBRE
10	1	0	0	1.5	0	0	0

Meringue is normally one of the hardest recipes to get right, let alone without using sugar. The basic principles still apply here: sound, clean, grease-free equipment; whites weighed and at room temperature for a better structure. The only difference here is that you whisk over a high speed until light and glossy but not too firm. They also cook much quicker than conventional meringues, so keep an eye out while they're in the oven. Once the meringues are cooked, they can be stored uncovered, and they will not weep or go soggy. I use a powdered sucralose sugar substitute rather than a granular one.

3 egg medium whites (97–100g),
  at room temperature
pinch of cream of tartar
15g powdered sugar substitute
  (such as Splenda)
½ teaspoon vanilla extract

Preheat the oven to 140°C/gas 1 and line a baking tray.

Place the egg whites and cream of tartar into the clean, grease-free bowl of an electric mixer, then place on the machine and whisk at a medium speed until soft and foamy.

Stop the machine and sprinkle over the sugar substitute and add the vanilla. Remove the whisk from the machine and use it as a hand whisk to just mix together the whites with the sugar substitute and vanilla. Place the whisk back on the machine and whisk at a high speed until thick, glossy and firm.

Pipe or spoon the meringue into the shape you require on the baking tray. Bake in the oven for 25–30 minutes, or until just coloured and firm to the touch. Cool and eat.

HALF-COOKED CHOCOLATE MERINGUE

£3.11

A nice, easy chocolate recipe here: I use 70 per cent cocoa chocolate but 90 per cent can be used if you want a darker, deeper taste. I have reduced the sugar content to only 100 grams in total, so if serving four it's only 25 grams each. I add a little extra melted chocolate to pour over and a light dusting of icing sugar, which are all completely optional. A small spoon of reduced-fat crème fraîche can also be served alongside.

MAKES	PREP TIME	COOK TIME	ENERGY (KCALS)	PROTEIN	FAT	SATURATED FAT	CARB.	TOTAL SUGARS	SALT	FIBRE
4	20 MINS	10-12 MINS	466	11	23	12	53	50	0.25	2

4 medium eggs, at room temperature

pinch of cream of tartar

100g caster sugar

2 level tablespoons cornflour, sieved

200g bitter chocolate (minimum 70% cocoa solids), melted

oil (in a spray bottle)

To serve

50g bitter chocolate, melted (or white is good)

cocoa powder (optional)

icing sugar (optional)

Preheat the oven to 230°C/gas 8.

Separate the eggs into whites and yolks; you only need two yolks for this dish. Whisk the egg whites with the cream of tartar in an electric mixer fitted with the whisk attachment on a medium speed until foamy and thick. Add the sugar and whisk until thick and glossy, taking your time.

Remove from the machine, and carefully fold in the two egg yolks, the cornflour and the melted chocolate. Spray a warmed 20cm ovenproof, non-stick frying pan with a little oil. Add the meringue mix and place the whole thing into the oven. Cook for 10–12 minutes, or until nicely risen and still just slightly undercooked in the middle.

Remove from the oven and immediately spoon over the melted chocolate. Serve dusted with a little cocoa powder and/or icing sugar, if using. Place the pan in the centre of the table and dig in.

TIP

Not only is dark chocolate a strong source of antioxidants, but also it is believed to reduce the risk of cardiovascular problems and lower cholesterol – but the darker the better, as it's the cocoa in chocolate that contains these benefits.

INDEX